Introdu...
Educati...

Introduction to Educational Psychology

E. Hendrikz

© E. Hendrikz, 1986

All rights reserved. No reproduction, copy or transmission
of this publication may be made without written permission.
No paragraph of this publication may be reproduced, copied
or transmitted save with written permission or in accordance
with the provisions of the Copyright Act 1956 (as amended).
Any person who does any unauthorised act in relation to
this publication may be liable to criminal prosecution and
civil claims for damages.

First published 1986

Published by *Macmillan Publishers Ltd*
London and Basingstoke
*Associated companies and representatives in Accra,
Auckland, Delhi, Dublin, Gaborone, Hamburg, Harare,
Hong Kong, Kuala Lumpur, Lagos, Manzini, Melbourne,
Mexico City, Nairobi, New York, Singapore, Tokyo*

ISBN 0–333–40900–0

Printed in Hong Kong

British Library Cataloguing in Publication Data
Hendrikz, E.
  Introduction to educational psychology. —
  (Macmillan international college editions)
  1. Educational psychology
  I. Title
  370.15   LB1051
ISBN 0–333–40900–0

Contents

Preface		vii
1	To the student	1
2	What is educational psychology?	8
3	The uniqueness of each human being	18
4	Common trends in development and learning	38
5	The developing child	49
6	Helping learning to take place	73
7	More about how our thinking and learning abilities develop	88
8	Some ways in which ideas about thinking and learning can influence educational methods and provision	111
9	The school's role in developing healthy personalities	118
10	Discipline and the school's responsibility for moral development	133
11	Understanding yourself as a teacher	149
12	Educational assessment	160
13	Guidance and counselling, the role of the teacher and the school	178
14	Psychology and the curriculum	189
Index		205

Application Exercises

Number	page	Number	page	Number	page
1	6	9	40	17	148
2	6	10	41	18	152
3	10	11	70	19	176
4	13	12	87	20	177
5	14	13	109	21	188
6	19	14	117	22	189
7	22	15	130	23	203
8	34	16	138		

Acknowledgements

The author and publishers wish to acknowledge, with thanks, the following photographic sources:
Format   p 35 (photo Margaret Murray)
John and Penny Hubley   pp 36 top; 77; 78
Middle East Pictures and Publicity   pp 36 bottom; 63; 82; cover

The publishers have made every effort to trace the copyright holders, but if they have inadvertently overlooked any, they will be pleased to make the necessary arrangements at the first opportunity.

Preface

One of the more influential educators in America, Ned Flanders[1], wrote that it was a serious indictment of the teaching profession to hear so many teacher-trainers say that their students would appreciate what they were learning in college only after they had had some practical experience of teaching. Matters were made much worse, he said, when the same teacher-trainers would then give a lecture on the importance of presenting the material to be learned in such a way that it would appeal to the immediate needs and interests of the pupils. They were preaching one thing to their students but practising something different. He went on to emphasise that the best way to understand educational ideas and concepts is to first try them out in real situations, what he called 'field experiences'. Once the student has had experience of them in the field he needs to look at the theory which lies behind them and make sure that he fully understands it. At present, Flanders wrote, the gap between educational theory and its practice is growing deeper and wider, often because the people whose job it is to narrow the gap are in fact extending it.

Nowhere in the process of teacher education is Flanders' accusation truer than in the field of educational psychology. All too often the psychology programme in departments and colleges of education consists of lectures, seminars and readings based on theoretical ideas thought to be essential for teachers to understand if they are to have a basis on which to plan successful learning experiences for their pupils. The selected topics and ideas are in most cases well chosen because they do, indeed, provide a necessary theoretical basis from which students and teachers can work, *if* they manage to see practical classroom uses for the theory, as well as to find sound theoretical bases for their classroom observation and experience. Good tutors of educational psychology illustrate the important ideas with examples drawn from teaching, and, when helping their students during teaching practice, will remind them of, for example, the need to plan for individual differences in learning ability. Nevertheless it is a fairly rare experience for students to have the necessary psychological knowledge and their practical teaching brought together in a direct way, so that psychology can help them to plan and organize successful teaching.

In educational theory, the gap between theory and practice to which Flanders refers lies not only in the methods often used in a teachers' college or other training course. It all too frequently also lies in the wide gap between the illustrations and research evidence used to help students to understand the necessary ideas, and the cultures and groups whom they will actually teach. Nowhere is this more true than in the so-called Third World Countries in Africa and elsewhere. The psychology most often taught is, understandably, taken from research and experience from Northern Hemisphere countries and the textbooks written for students in those countries. Often these textbooks do include chapters on the influence of different cultures on development and learning which, if taken further, could form a basis for understanding local circumstances. But their overall starting point is Western, for which they cannot be blamed. The fault lies not so much in the textbooks themselves, as in the way in which they are used in teacher training institutions, the biggest error lying in the common practice of requiring students to start with the text and perhaps work towards a local interpretation. This is a complete reversal of the proven principle of learning which shows that first hand experience must come before students can fully understand and use general principles in their teaching. The result is that in the minds of many student teachers, educational psychology is a subject studied for its own sake rather than as a source of tools for immediate use in the classroom. They are lucky indeed if as teachers, they eventually understand and make use of even a small portion of what they studied from textbooks and in lectures during their initial training course. If the psychology they have studied has paid only little attention to local circumstances but remained firmly rooted in a distant and relatively unfamiliar world, they will be even less likely to be able to make conscious use of any of its teachings in their own work, even after they have had practical experience; very little of what they have learned will have remained with them as anything more than a few hazy memories.

It is now time that something was said in defence of those responsible for teaching educational psychology in non-Western countries. Firstly, because of the enormous expansion in the provision of schooling and the resultant need for large numbers of teachers, many new training colleges have been built and existing ones enlarged. Staff appointed to these colleges often have had very little opportunity, since their own professional training courses, to study psychology from the viewpoint of a teacher trainer. Where further study has been undertaken more formally it is often done in a Western rather than in a local context and hence reinforces its unfamiliar aspects. Even when the influence of culture on child development and learning has been included in such study, it is likely to have been too general, drawing on research from many different cultures, and so not of immediate benefit in their locality, where material is limited. It is small wonder that great reliance is placed on a set textbook and the emphasis of the students' study localised only to a limited extent.

Secondly, increased numbers of students leads to larger groups being taught in colleges and being supervised and tutored in practical teaching in schools. The opportunities for the psychology tutor, or indeed any college tutor, to help individual students to use the findings of psychology in their own work are very small and their supervising class teachers rarely have enough theoretical knowledge to undertake this task. Thirdly, but linked to the previous two points, planning an educational psychology course which includes frequent and carefully ordered observation and work with suitable children is very difficult to achieve even in the most advanced school system. In the situation existing in most developing countries it is small wonder that the teaching of educational psychology tends to remain even more academic and bookish than it does in more favourable situations.

This book, then, represents an attempt to go at least a little way towards bringing the lessons of psychology into the classroom practice of teachers. It is written primarily with the student himself[2] in mind and includes not only descriptive illustrations of typical events and situations which require some knowledge of educational psychology for their efficient handling, but also practical observations and exercises for the student to undertake. In many instances the task can and should be made easier by the college tutor or school authorities who can arrange for the necessary direct experience. It is hoped that the college course is so planned that opportunities occur at intervals throughout its length to work with children, individually, in small groups and in whole classes. Well motivated students should be able to take advantage on their own initiative of these opportunities, and of others occurring in their home areas during vacations, to add to the first hand experience of children and learning situations.

Although the book is written with the needs of the students in mind it is not intended to be a complete self-study programme. Even if it were possible to use the book in this way, it would not be adviseable. For example, although all student teachers need to have some general knowledge of child-development and learning principles at all ages and levels, they need greater depth and detail in the area in which they are most likely to teach, pre-school, primary, secondary, etc. Whenever possible, the book suggests particular exercises for such special areas. But it should be the task of tutors to add further depth, both practical and theoretical, in these areas. Then, too, no book can include all possible local variations in symptoms and circumstances; the best it can do is to lead students to general psychological principles which must be interpreted and adapted to make sense of their own situations. Perhaps tutors will find something in it to help them add direct relevance to their students' study.

The purpose of this book, then, is to introduce student teachers to essential aspects of educational psychology by starting with real situations and moving from there into some essential theorising. It makes no pretence of being comprehensive to the extent that many textbooks on educational psychology are; for those students and teachers who wish to explore a topic further there are suggestions for reading. Putting the objectives of the book into more or less practical (sometimes called 'behavioural') terms, by the end of the course the student should be able to:

a) plan his curriculum and his teaching in accordance with the most likely psychological circumstances of the learners;
b) ensure that each individual in his classes learns to the extent of his ability in the light of the best available psychological principles;
c) ensure that each pupil is enabled to continue full and balanced development, making use of knowledge of general human trends and reactions which influence individual and group behaviour;
d) solve the commoner educational problems likely to be met in the early stages of a teaching career;
e) understand those of his own motives and attitudes which might influence his approach to his professional responsibilities and practices;
f) continue to develop his teaching competence both by drawing on psychological principles already in his possession and by extending them by further reading and observation.

Notes

1 Flanders, N.E., 1963. 'Intent, interaction and feedback: a preparation for teaching', in *Journal of Teacher Education*, 14, pp 251-260.
2 For convenience the masculine form is used throughout the book; there is no sinister implication for female students and teachers.

CHAPTER ONE

To the student

The author expects that most users of this book will be students who are setting out on a course to prepare them for the profession of teaching. They may be full-time students in a College of Education or similar institution or they may be members of the increasingly common in-service courses in which short periods of full-time study alternate with periods of full-time paid teaching in a school, combined with part-time study.

Whichever is the pattern of the particular course of which you are a member, you will soon find that you need to spend a considerable amount of time studying on your own outside the timetabled periods which your tutors have planned for you, not just to ensure that you can pass the necessary examinations but, more importantly, so that you will be able to become a better teacher because you have understood and are able to use, in real life situations, the knowledge that you have gained. This book is designed to give you more guidance than do most textbooks on how to learn what you need to know of educational psychology so that it can be of direct and practical value in your profession.

The decision to design the book in the way that it is designed is based on several important principles, most, if not all, of which are of direct use to you in making sure that your own pupils learn sucessfully. First of all, learning is most successful when the learner is *actively involved* with the material to be learned in as many different ways as possible. Think, for example, what happens in a lecture. If it is interesting and clearly presented, you, as a member of the audience, may be mentally very active, listening carefully, trying to identify the important points, perhaps taking notes or trying to compare what you are hearing with your own experience. But research has shown that if you do not follow up the lecture with such activities as discussing the topic with others, writing fuller notes, thinking about it and finding out

1

more on your own, comparing the lecturer's ideas with those that you already have and so on, you will very soon forget a great deal of what the lecture contained. You, the learner, are not sufficiently actively involved in making the new knowledge and ideas part of yourself. If this is the fate of the content of good lectures, listened to with real effort, how much less useful are average and poor lectures and students who are only averagely interested and active.

Think, too, of what your experience is of reading a straightforward textbook. Students often say that they find it difficult to learn from books, even though they are very competent intellectually and in their language comprehension. In most cases they are surprised to find that this is a fairly common problem, resulting from the expectation that one should always be able to understand and remember the facts and ideas presented in a textbook on first reading it through. A second and third slow and deliberate reading is often necessary, the reader consciously making sure that he has understood its full meaning and finding personal examples to clarify it wherever possible. But even this amount of activity on the part of the learner may not be enough to ensure that the important parts of the content do not become too blurred after a short time to be of real use. Successful students involve themselves in many other activities, such as summarising the content and ideas in their own words, as far as possible without looking back at the text, going over the material in their own minds later in the same day, discussing it with fellow students, comparing the author's ideas with those of others, finding examples and illustrations from other sources and so on. All these are important activities which will enable the student to remember what he has read, because he has fully understood it and actively and consciously fitted the new facts and ideas into his existing mental store of related material, rather like putting another piece of a jigsaw puzzle into its right place and thus making more sense of the whole picture.

But activity, even of the sort suggested above, is not in itself enough to ensure that the *right sort of learning* takes place. The learner must also be helped to discover and be very clear about the purpose of the learning and what he should be able to use it for. For example, if the purpose of someone reading a book about car engines is to make him better able to maintain his own car in a serviceable state, he would not normally read a highly technical book intended for the graduate engineer, swallowing great quantities of theory about the internal combustion engine. He would select material which would give him practical information about how to ensure that his engine oil is clean, his tyres at the right pressure and the spark plugs and hoses in good condition, and he would examine the relevant parts of the car to put into practice what he has read in the book. A good student would probably go a bit further and realise that he would get better performance from his car if he understood some of the underlying reasons for maintaining particular parts of the car and how each part fits into the whole to make the engine work properly. He would expect to be better able to make decisions about the car with a more general knowledge gained from a sensible mixture of practice and theory.

These principles and others, which should become clearer later on, are the ones on which this book is based. Just as you, when you are a teacher, will plan a variety of activities for your pupils to help them to achieve the necessary learning, so does this book attempt to involve *you* in a variety of learning activities. This is done not merely because the planned activity will help you to understand and remember the content in a theoretical way. It is also done because at this stage of your career what you need is a basis of *practical* understanding of your pupils, their similarities and differences, how their development is progressing and what to expect of them, how they can best be helped to learn both from the more formal content of their curriculum and from their wider school experience. Just as the person needing to know about his car should spend a lot of time investigating the car itself to make the contents of the handbook real and usable, so should a student who is preparing himself for the profession of teaching spend a lot of time taking the ideas and information that the textbook offers into real and personal situations.

There is yet another justification for this approach, especially in the area of educational psychology and that is that, although there are well-established general principles of human behaviour and development, there is very considerable variation, not only from individual to individual but also from group to group and culture to culture. This is a theme which will run strongly through this book. No textbook can begin to answer in detail the many questions about his pupils and his work which a teacher must constantly ask himself. All it can do by itself is to suggest possibilities, likely explanations, information that should be sought from the particular situation that he finds himself in, etc. For this reason alone, teachers and prospective teachers should learn their basic psychology while in contact with the people to whom it must be applied. All the time, principles and ideas in the text should be translated by the student into locally relevant circumstances, the statements made compared with his own observations and their implications for himself and his work identified.

You will then see that this text is intended as a starting point rather than as a source of all necessary knowledge. It is a starting point, not only for the development of your own professional ability but also for a more detailed study of special aspects of educational psychology which will help you to develop a deeper understanding of your pupils, yourself, your work and so on. Throughout the book, practical activities are suggested for you to undertake. These are designed both to help you to understand more clearly the important psychological and educational principles described and to give you an opportunity to see how far they apply to your own pupils or the children in your own community. Until you have achieved these insights you are not very likely to be able to use the information which the text offers to help you to teach effectively and to solve satisfactorily the very many problems which are a major part of a teacher's work.

How, then, can you make the best use of this book? There is no single or simple answer to this question because there is so much variation between individual study needs and circumstances. It is very likely, for example, that you are using the book as part of a course offered in a College of Education or similar institution. It is hoped that your tutors will give you a sense of direction through the book and its proposed activities. They may even require you to present formal records of at least some of the activities, as an integral part of your course. It is strongly recommended, as part of your personal study programme (whether or not it is actually required of you) that you keep a file into which you can put your own notes, answers to the questions posed and observations and conclusions, both those derived from a careful study of the text itself and those proposed in the recommended activities. Such a file should also include notes and references to related material and ideas which you come across in your further reading or even accidentally in your day-to-day observations. Disciplining yourself to do this, even if no one in authority checks up on it, is sound practice for efficient study, not only of educational psychology but also of most other subjects. Further, it is essential if your self-study is to make a real impact on your teaching, that you make a *conscious* effort to note what use you make, or have made, of the information you have gained from it in the classroom itself. The study of educational psychology in an initial training course for teachers is largely a waste of time if it is not used on the job as a major tool; but making the jump from theory to practice and back to theory again is a most difficult one to achieve. Your college course is almost certainly designed to help you to do this and your tutors undoubtedly do all that they can to make the theory real, but in the last resort most of the responsibility lies with you. Used properly , it is hoped that this book will help you to develop habits of relating theory to practice, of questioning the theory if it does not fit your own experience and of looking at the work of other authors to expand your present knowledge. It should also help you to see your pupils as individuals who can be understood to some extent in the light of general psychological principles but who deserve your consideration and concern on their own account and who will certainly not conform completely to any preconceived pattern.

Another question that you are likely to ask, especially if you have to study on your own to any extent, is how fast you should go through the book. If you complete the proposed activities conscientiously you are not likely to be able to rush through it. A general good, rule to follow is to work relatively slowly, returning to a topic at intervals over a period of time, thinking about it at odd moments so that you can give yourself a chance to digest the ideas and make them part of your existing knowledge. This is a process which cannot be hurried but, as with most other things, there are great individual differences, both in the ease with which individuals absorb and use new ideas and in the complexity of the ideas themselves. Only you can judge when you are ready to move on to a new topic and even when you have gone further through the book it will probably be necessary for you to return to an earlier section, especially when you meet a new aspect or illustration of an old principle. You will find that to some extent later topics depend on a clear understanding of earlier ones so that it is probably best to follow the logical progression built into the text. This principle, however, should not be too rigidly kept to because the process of educating the young requires a mixing of many different aspects of psychological knowledge and you may find the need for information covered later rather than earlier. The important point is that if your study approaches have been successful you will be continually adding to the knowledge you already have, the new ideas often making you alter some of the old and revise your approach to teaching.

Application 1

This chapter has already given you some ideas about how people can be helped to learn. Although the purpose was to suggest study techniques for you, some important general principles have been outlined which apply to all ages and to much of the learning that you will have to plan for your own pupils.

Look back over this chapter and write down the principles of learning which you have been able to identify so far. Then turn to the end of the chapter and compare your list with the suggested one.

Application 2

Arrange to watch at least one whole lesson with any age of children. Make notes of everything the teacher expects the children to *do* in order to ensure that they learn what is required. The table at the end of this chapter will suggest a useful way of doing this; it proposes that you describe each activity briefly under the most appropriate principle.

Important note

Be sure to explain what you are doing to the teacher whom you are watching, making it clear that you are not in any way criticising his or her lesson but are trying to understand more clearly how successful learning is achieved, by analysis and observation of successful lessons. If possible, discuss your analysis with the class teacher or with fellow students watching the same lesson.

Notes

Application 1

Did you identify the following principles?

(i) The learning intended in the lesson should be extended and reinforced by further activity of the learner outside the timetable.

(ii) The teacher (or text book author) should give guidance on *how* to learn the material.

(iii) The learner himself should be quite clear about what is expected of him and where the new learning fits into his previous knowledge. He should also feel that it is related to his own life needs.

(iv) The learner should himself be actively involved in the learning in as many different ways as possible, for example practising the skill, discussing with others, making notes, answering questions which require him to think for himself, making models, diagrams and pictures, writing stories, etc.

(v) The teacher should be quite clear exactly what he wants the pupils to learn (i.e. the *learning objectives*) and must plan so that he can identify, at the end of the time, what has been learned.

Some teachers plan their learning objectives by beginning their preparation of each lesson with a statement such as: 'By the end of the lesson all the pupils should be able to ...' followed by a detailed statement of what they should be able to do, or be better able to do as a result of the lesson. The author has done this in the final paragraph of the Preface to this book.

Application 2

I suggest that you turn a sheet of paper sideways and draw five columns to correspond with the five principles shown in Application 1, and try briefly to describe what learning activities were undertaken during the lesson.

(i)	(ii)	(iii)	(iv)	(v)

Further reading

Since one of the purposes of this chapter is to help you to improve your own learning techniques, both for your own sake and because it should give you more insight into how your pupils learn, you would find it useful to read one of the several books available on how to study.

You would find it useful to look at the general educational psychology texts on your college shelves and read what is said about the importance of learning objectives and how to identify them. The index may list them under the heading, *Behavioural Objectives,* or *Objectives in Learning* or even under *Learning Objectives*. A good example is: Vander Zanden, J.W., *Educational Psychology in Theory and Practice*, New York, Random House, 1980, pp 322 to 329.

CHAPTER TWO

What is educational psychology?

So far we have used the term *educational psychology* without explaining what it is or why teachers need to know something about it in order to do their work properly. You have already gathered from the previous discussion that it has a contribution to make to successful learning and teaching.

Psychology is the science that studies people in order to discover how and why they develop in the way that they do. It tries to find common patterns, or principles, as well as to identify the circumstances which emphasise the differences between individuals in their behaviour, abilities, interests and so on. Psychologists aim at building up a body of knowledge about people so that it will become increasingly possible to predict, within broad limits, how people *will* behave, how to influence them and how to help them to develop in the best way.

Educational psychology is a special branch of the whole science of psychology. Think for a few minutes of what a teacher's job is, and what knowledge he will need to have about his pupils in order to do it successfully. We have already introduced you to some principles which enable learning to take place; there are many more. These have been identified and tested by psychologists and turned into useful 'tools' for the non-psychologist to use. But, as we shall see, the teacher's job is a great deal more than ensuring that his pupils learn the content of the curriculum or the syllabus. For example, a teacher is often expected to help his pupils to continue to develop into individuals who will be useful adults in society and who have the necessary personal qualities and abilities to enable them to make healthy social adjustments. Every individual has different potential abilities and a teacher should be able to work alongside his home, family, neighbourhood and community to see that each of his pupils has a chance to develop as well as he possibly can. You will probably discuss more fully in other parts of your teacher training course what schools and teachers are expected to do for their pupils. It is important that you make conscious efforts to analyse the ideas which you meet, especially those which apply specifically to your own country or area and make notes, to keep in your educational psychology file, of what the teacher needs to know about his pupils and about child development and the learning process if he is to become a good practitioner.

Let us look at some examples of educational aims that schools and teachers are often expected to fulfill and try to identify the knowledge derived from psychology which teachers will need to have. The purposes of education usually fall into three categories:
(i) *Knowledge and Skills*, such as being able to read, handle numbers, pass tests and examinations in the subjects in the curriculum, etc.;
(ii) *Personal and Social Traits* such as honesty, responsibility, loyalty, co-operation, etc.;
(iii) *Intellectual or Cognitive Skills* such as the ability to make sensible decisions based on sound reasoning, to be able to continue to learn new things once one has left formal schooling behind, etc.

In order to achieve the purposes suggested in category (i) above, the teacher needs to be able to draw on the science of psychology for answers to questions such as:
a) Have all people the same capacity to learn? If not, what causes the difference and what can teachers do to help all to achieve to the best of their ability?
b) Do all people learn the same thing in the same way or is there variation between individuals? What are the differences and what can a teacher do about it?
c) Is there a difference in the sort of material that can be learned by children at different ages as well as with different abilities? If so what does this mean as far as successful teaching is concerned?
d) Is there a relationship between children's home circumstances and experiences and the level of success they achieve in learning in school? If so, what is this and what must be done about it by the teacher?
e) Is there a relationship between the cultural and ethnic background from which children come and the ways in which they can best be helped to learn?

These are enough for the moment, since the purpose at present is to convince you that a study of educational psychology is essential to a teacher because it can help him to identify both the questions which he must ask about his pupils and the answers to many of them which should provide clues to help him achieve success.

Application 3

Write down at least four questions to which you think a teacher will need to have psychologically-based answers if he is to achieve his aim in categories (ii) and (iii).

Turn to the end of this chapter and compare your ideas with those listed there. Do not be surprised if you have some suggestions different from the author's. It is impossible, and at present unnecessary, to give a really complete list. Make a note to look again at this section when you have completed the course of the book. Can you now give fairly satisfactory answers to your own questions and those which I have suggested?

More value will be gained from this exercise if you work with a small group of fellow students, comparing notes, discussing ideas with your tutor, etc.

The scope of educational psychology

Here is a summary of areas where educational psychology can provide a foundation on which a teacher can build his work. But it must be said at the outset that psychologists do not claim to have answers to every question that a teacher will need to ask about his pupils and how to do his best for them. Human beings are such complex creatures that it is impossible to identify rules of development which apply to them all. The most that psychologists can claim is that a teacher has a better chance of being successful in his work if he is familiar with, and takes into consideration, the findings from research and observations than if he approaches his work haphazardly. Psychology is a fairly new science and its findings are constantly being extended, tested, refined and modified. Because of the flexible and changing state of psychology, as well as the incredible complexity of human beings, a teacher must develop the habit of looking realistically at himself and his own pupils to help him to decide how psychology can best be applied in his particular situation. In a sense he must himself become a psychologist, in that he must study his actual pupils and their educational and personal needs in their real situations. He must, as do all true scientists, test the rules proposed by others to see whether they fit present facts and experiment with possible solutions to problems to obtain the best results. Educational psychology can help him to identify the questions he must ask himself about his pupils and give clues as to where to look for answers and what actions are most likely to lead to success.

As we shall see, psychology deals with probabilities and likelihoods rather than certainties, but this is not a reason for rejecting its findings. Equally, a study of psychology as a theoretical subject, learned from books and tested by written examinations to see how thoroughly the facts as stated are remembered and understood, is of very little real help in itself to the teacher in the classroom. He needs to build up a *useable* set of psychological principles and possibilities which can help him to understand his own pupils. Without constant interaction between the theory and the practice he is not very likely to be able to use the valuable teaching tools which psychology can provide for him.

Areas where educational psychology can help the teacher

1 *Finding patterns of growth and development which are common to all normal human beings.*
These are looked at from several viewpoints, the physical, intellectual (or cognitive), social and emotional and their interactions which make up the whole personality. If there were no general patterns of behaviour and development common to all normal human beings, so that everyone developed in a completely individual and random way, the teacher's job would be virtually impossible; indeed, human society would probably not exist, and neither, probably, would human beings.

A teacher needs to know at least in general terms what abilities and behaviours pupils are likely to have attained at various ages to give an indication as to where to start looking for individual variation. He also needs to know what is the likely direction that development will take so that he can help them along their natural route.

2 *Finding the range and scope of the variation in growth and development which individuals show, within the general pattern.*
This must include not merely an understanding of the existence

of such variabilty but also the factors which seem to cause it, or at least to be related to it in some way. The teacher needs the knowledge in this area for two main reasons. Firstly, he needs a starting point from which to identify the likely individual variations among his pupils and then to be able to make allowances for them. Secondly, he needs to know how far and in what ways he can influence the development and behaviour of each of his pupils.

3 *Stressing that each individual pupil is also an integral part of his wider family, social and cultural group who can be fully educated only in the light of knowledge of that background.*
The purpose of education is not to separate pupils from their families, neighbourhoods and cultures but rather to help them to become fuller and more valuable members of their culture groups. This is especially important among those groups which place great value on strong family and community ties and obligations, as do many developing countries. It is important that, while aiming at developing each individual's potential abilities and qualities to the full, teachers must do all that they can to treat them as also being inseparable parts of their own families and wider backgrounds.

4 *Indentifying principles which research and experience show promote learning.*
Some of these, of course, are found in the areas described in paragraphs 1 and 2 above; but there are many more which, if taken consciously into account, will help the teacher to succeed in his task of enabling his pupils to learn not only the content of the curriculum but also the human and social skills which healthy, well-balanced people need. An aspect of education, often overlooked by teachers in their curriculum and lesson planning, is how they teach their pupils *how to learn*; the emphasis is almost exclusively on *what they shall learn*. An understanding and conscious use of learning principles are essential to achieve this important goal of education. You will, I hope, see that the structure of this book is planned to enable you to learn educational psychology for your purposes. Teaching your pupils and yourself how to learn will, if successful, develop attitudes and habits which will be of life-long use in learning situations. The psychology of learning is an important contributor to your bag of professional tools.

5 *Understanding oneself both as a person and as a teacher.*
Strictly speaking the 'person' and the 'teacher' should not be considered separately because they are inseparable. On the other hand, all of us, while being unique individuals with our own sets of abilities and disabilities, interests, motives and attitudes, combine within ourselves different proportions and strengths of the qualities which make up our whole selves. The actual mixture which is shown is altered to suit the particular activity which we happen to be engaged in at the time. We are all, at one time or another in our lives, different people in relation to others. We are a son or daughter, a brother or sister, a colleague or classmate, a parent, an aunt, uncle or other relative, a customer, an employer and a great many other things. In each of these relationships, while remaining the same person, we draw on different aspects of our basic selves. The role of *teacher* is the one with which we are most concerned here.

A study of educational psychology can help you to look at yourself realistically, which will in turn help you to see yourself as your pupils see you. Are you someone who frightens them without meaning to or are you someone whom they can trust? What situations in school make you angry or happy and why? Why are you entering the teaching profession? The study of psychology can help you to identify at least some of the answers to questions which you should ask yourself and to realize the importance of the answers for the pupils whom you will teach. It can also help you to make happy professional relationships with colleagues and, because of the greater insight into yourself that you will have, will help you to understand your pupils and those most important people, their parents, more fully.

In the following application exercises there are no right or wrong answers. They are intended to focus your attention on situations which illustrate some of the psychological principles which we shall study in more detail later. It is hoped, too, that they will be the beginning of habits of observation and questioning in you whenever the opportunity arises.

Application 4

Arrange, preferably with a fellow student, to spend at least one lesson in a class with a teacher (on a different occasion from Application 2). Describe the situations in which the teacher appears:
a) to deal with the class as though the children were the same as each other and able to do the same things in the same way;

b) to deal with individuals or small groups as though they were different from other individuals or groups. This might be in his or her expectations about the children's basic knowledge, learning ability, interests, length of time during which they can concentrate on one task, length of time it takes them to complete a task and any other aspect of the lesson.

Discuss your observations as soon as possible afterwards with the least one fellow student. If that fellow student observed the same lesson, so much the better. In your opinion, and without presuming to evaluate the class teacher, how justified was he or she in assuming similarities and differences and catering for them? In other words, how successful was the learning of most pupils?

Application 5

Imagine that you were a pupil in the class which you observed in Application 4. Describe the teacher as you would see him or her. By this I do not mean in physical appearance but in personality and attitudes to the class and individual pupils within it. How do you think the pupils *feel* about him or her as their teacher?

Why educational psychology for Third World and multi-cultural education systems?

This book is intended primarily to prepare teachers who will work in countries which have only fairly recently become independent, or unified under a central government and hence are faced with the problem of developing a wide-ranging and modern education system, often from very rudimentary foundations. A number of labels have been attached to such countries, the commonest being 'developing', which implies that until recently there have been barriers to the establishment of a modern state in which everyone has a reasonable physical standard of living and access to educational and health facilities.

There are economic implications as well, suggesting the need for an increasingly sophisticated economy which can interact with those of other countries. The demand for rapid economic and social change is a characteristic of such countries. Hence, a focal point in their governments' policies is the development of new systems and institutions and the modification of existing ones to fulfill, in as short a time as possible, the requirements of the country, both as identified by planners and as expected by the electorate.

Sometimes such countries can also be described as 'multi-cultural', or 'plural'. While multi-cultural and plural societies do not necessarily also warrant the description 'developing' in terms of the previous paragraph, the latter are often characterised by the wide range of diversity among their inhabitants. This characteristic is a very important one for teachers and one which cannot be satisfactorily managed by educators without the awareness created by a study of educational psychology, which itself must include social psychology. They may indeed be multi-cultural in the sense that there are several distinct ethnic, religious and linguistic groups within their borders, a state being increasingly called 'plural'. But they may also be 'multi-cultural' in the sense that, even in a single ethnic and language group, there is a wide economic, educational and social range which will have to be taken into account, especially in the educational sphere.

The multi-cultural and plural nature of most developing countries has many dimensions. There is the matter of ethnicity itself, and of sub-groupings within a single ethnic group which have resulted in divergence of language, customs, values, religious practices, attitudes to children and their discipline, the status of women *vis-à-vis* men, relationships within families and the sort of families which are most common (polygamous, extended, monogamous, nuclear, etc.). Cutting across these broader divisions, other differences include socio-economic status, ranging from the minimally educated peasant living in remote areas and with little access to the cash economy or modern technology, to the well-travelled, highly-educated and sophisticated business or professional person. There is the new generation of urban dweller, many of whom are compelled to accept unskilled industrial or commercial work and who, because of the size of the influx from the rural to the urban areas, often live in sub-standard and overcrowded housing. Yet another dimension is a generational one, often much wider in developing than in the so-called developed countries, because of the rapidity of change. All too often, children are even further away from their parents' generation than children are alleged to be in older-established countries, and change is so rapid that this gap will increase, becoming significant for the teachers themselves, many of whom will have experienced the generation gap between themselves and their parents, but who could also increasingly experience it between themselves and their pupils.

What, then, are the implications for education of the wide variety and great speed of change which teachers in education systems in developing countries are more likely to meet in their extreme form than will teachers in longer established systems? It is increasingly being realised that a great many aspects of a child's environment and experience have a direct influence on the development of its abilities, motives, ambitions and its attitudes towards school and learning. Urban children often do better in school than do rural children, partly because many schools fail to take into account their differing experiences and backgrounds. There may be differences in the way that boys and girls are brought up and in the things that they are expected to be able to do, and this could influence their school success if they are not taken into account by the teacher. Another important influence on school achievement is the quality of the language used at home, even if it is the same one as that used in the school. When the language of the school and home differ, so that the children are learning in a second language, the problems are multiplied and even more so when the teacher himself is having to use a second language.

All the foregoing and the many other examples which could have been mentioned, occur in most schools and educational districts, in developed as well as in developing countries. The difference lies in the extent and strength of the range of variation and in the speed of change taking place, both as a result of population movements and of time itself. These are very much greater and hence more important in developing and multi-cultural countries than in older more static ones and teachers in the former will need to be exceptionally well aware of the importance of understanding the pupils whom they will teach and modifying their methods and expectations to fit the realities of the situation. They will also need to understand themselves and their own need to retain flexibility and adaptability throughout their careers. All teachers in all countries should possess these qualities; teachers in developing and multi-cultural ones have even greater challenges in these areas. The study of psychology, especially if it leads to a deeply rooted sensitivity towards the needs of the pupils as they really are, is essential for the teacher. It is important, then, that teachers who expect to work where there are many of the more common problems of a developing country, should be helped to study psychology in their own contexts, interpreting general principles through local examples and using them in their own teaching.

Notes

Application 3

Here are some possible questions which you may have identified as needing knowledge gained from a study of psychology. It would be useful to refer to them occasionally, as you work through this book, to see whether you have answers which will be of practical value to you in your teaching.

Personal and social traits
1 Can a teacher and a school actually influence the development of such traits? If so, how?
2 Is there a difference in what can be expected of children at different ages? If so, what are the most important ones?
3 What individual differences can be expected in the effectiveness with which these traits can be developed and what sort of factors seem to be related to the differences e.g. genetic, family attitudes and customs, cultural variation?

Intellectual and cognitive skills
1 How important is genetic inheritance in determining how well individuals learn?
2 How much reliance can be placed on the scores obtained in tests which are intended to measure intelligence?
3 In what ways can school experience improve or limit the development of intellectual ability?
4 Do the ways in which children think and reason change as they grow older or is there merely an increase in capacity while using the same thinking methods? If they change in their reasoning methods and skills, what are the changes and how can one recognise them?

Further reading

It is not too early to begin to develop your knowledge and ideas about the purposes of education in your country. I strongly recommend you to read Thompson, A.R., *Education and Development in Africa*, London Macmillan, 1981, pp. 3-123. I hope that you will go on further through the book as it will introduce you to educational ideas which can provide a context into which you can fit your understanding of educational psychology and child development.

CHAPTER THREE

The uniqueness of each human being

If the purpose of this book were to give you a neatly built up theoretical picture of human development and how, as a teacher, to influence it, the logical starting point would probably be a discussion of general principles and patterns of development, leading towards an examination of individual variations from the general, what causes them and how to deal with them. Since, however, this book is founded on the belief that a student undergoing initial teacher training can best develop a usable set of psychological tools by starting with firsthand experience in real situations, we must start from your particular experience and move towards useful generalisations. You cannot, then, proceed with your study until you have had a minimum of experience and undertaken the exercises set out here. Those of you who are studying while engaged in teaching have a considerable advantage over those who have less extensive and regular access to schools and children, but you could also put yourself at a disadvantage if you assume that because of your experience you can analyse the required data without looking afresh at your pupils and their performance, and answering the questions from your new observations.

All of us bring with us into our teaching, a collection of long-held ideas about schools, children, learning and so on which, often without our realising it, influence our actions and attitudes. This is why it is essential for anyone wishing to prepare himself for this most important profession to develop habits of honest, open observation and self-questioning. Teachers must not be content to accept, at their face value, statements and arguments without ensuring that they fit the circumstances as they really are. As an example, one often hears statements such as, 'All adolescents are difficult and moody people', or, 'Girls can't do higher mathematics'. In certain circumstances there may be some truth in statements such as these, but they must not be allowed to influence judgements and actions until a great deal more knowledge and personal observation has convinced us of their truth or otherwise.

Application 6

Arrange to spend sufficient time with ONE class of pupils, at any age level, to enable you to collect the following information. Do not expect to complete the exercise in a hour or so; it could stretch over several periods. Considerably greater benefit would be gained if you work with a fellow student or a small group, and discuss these and other observations with each other.

1 *Category of school* — primary, secondary, urban, rural, peri-urban, denominational, private fee paying, single or mixed sex etc.

2 *Class level chosen*
Is it streamed according to ability or is it of mixed ability? Single or mixed sex?

3 *Age range*
The youngest child is _____ years _____ months.
The oldest child is _____ years _____ months.

4 *Height*
The tallest boy is _____ (cms or feet and inches)
The tallest girl is _____
The shortest boy is _____
The shortest girl is _____

5 *Family size*
How many children are the only child in their family?
How many have between one and four brothers and sisters?
How many have more than four brothers and sisters?
How many are the youngest child in their family?
How many are the oldest child in their family?

6 *Reading ability*
Identify by your own observation and/or in consultation with the class teacher:
a) the best reader in the class,
b) the worst reader in the class.
Describe the most obvious differences between their reading skills.

7 *Home language*
How many pupils, when at home, speak a language different from the one in which they are being taught at school?

8 *Learning difficulties*
Which pupils appear to have difficulty in learning a subject (other

than reading) of your choice? Describe the difficulties as they appear to you.
9   *Physical handicaps*
Watch the pupils carefully and often.
   a) Are there any who seem to have difficulty in hearing clearly? (Some of the signs are: turning their heads to one side or straining them forward to listen, frequently mishearing, asking for instructions to be repeated, etc.)
   b) Are there any who seem to have difficulty in seeing clearly, whether or not they wear glasses? (Some of the signs are: screwing up the eyes and peering at a book or chalk board, holding reading matter close to the face, often mis-seeing words when reading and complaints of headaches.)
10 *Home background*
   a) How many pupils have fathers who hold professional jobs such as doctors, lawyers, teachers, engineers, accountants, business owners and managers?
   b) How many pupils have mothers who hold professional jobs?
   c) How many have fathers who are employed as skilled workers such as mechanics, clerks, bookkeepers, farmers, drivers, bricklayers, carpenters, plumbers?
   d) How many have mothers employed in skilled work such as nurses, secretaries, farmers, bookkeepers, clerks, drivers, sales representatives, shop assistants, etc.?
   e) How many have fathers employed in semi-skilled jobs such as messengers, labourers in factories, on roads, farms, etc.?

The foregoing observations have, I hope, helped you to focus on just a few of the ways in which pupils in the same class differ from one another, in areas which research and experience show can influence children's development and learning and thus must be understood by the teacher. There are many other ways in which people differ from each other and which are at least as important as the ones selected for this exercise. We shall be looking at some of them in more detail later. You will, I hope, have noticed that the areas for observation which were selected included:
(i) some with which people are born, such as age and physical height;
(ii) some which relate to the school organisation, such as class level and the basis on which children have been allocated to it (age, ability, sex).
(iii) some which relate to the pupils' actual achievements such as reading competence, particular learning difficulties;

(iv) some which relate to the geographical environment in which the school, if not the pupil's home, is situated (urban, peri-urban, rural).
(v) some which relate to the personal home circumstances of the pupils, such as position in the family, its size, home language, parents' occupations, etc.

You will not, with any certainty, be able to identify the reasons why any particular child succeeds or fails in learning to the extent that he does. Even highly qualified psychologists, with many tests available to them, are cautious when measuring capacities and achievements of individuals. In any case, there is rarely only one single cause of learning success or failure; usually several of them interact and reinforce or cancel one another out. It is important, however, that right from the start of your teaching career you are sensitive to the circumstances of each of your pupils so that you can build on strengths and make up for limitations. The need for such an attitude is emphasised when it is remembered that in the course of your career you may teach in several different schools in a variety of geographical, social and economic areas. These can range from rural areas remote from urban centres, where facilities in the schools may be limited, formal schooling relatively recent and many parents themselves unschooled, to well-established and equipped urban schools where the children come from mainly literate and economically comfortable homes. Other important variations to which you are likely to have to adapt include such things as the proportion of pupils in the schools who are learning in a language other than that of their homes and the inclusion in the class of children with different ethnic or cultural, backgrounds. There may even be variability between the two sexes, which in turn can differ from culture to culture and social group to social group, and teachers must be aware of this.

Once a teacher is aware of the major factors likely to influence the individual variations among his pupils, what should his attitude be? He certainly should not use any factor to excuse effort on his part. There are teachers who label children as 'unintelligent', or 'lazy' or 'from a poor home' and then make no effort to help that individual to develop whatever potential he has. A teacher's responsibility is to each pupil separately, even though, because of the realities of most school situations and the complexity of human beings, only rarely is it possible to cater satisfactorily for all of every individual's needs. But the effort must be made, the starting point for which is an honest attempt to find out as much as possible about each pupil. The aim is not to get rid of the individual differences, which in any case is impossible, but to reduce the underdevelopment and underachievement which can prevent individuals from success. If it seems that you, or any other teacher, has brought all his pupils to the same level of skill or knowledge, there is a need to look again, not necessarily at the less able but at the more able, to see if they could have advanced further.

Application 7

Plan a lesson which you will teach to a class of children, preferably the one which you observed and reported on in Application 6. The topic must be one which is suitable for the class but as far as possible plan that it shall contain some ideas, knowledge or skills which are new to the pupils. Specify at the beginning of your lesson plan exactly what you expect the pupils to be able to do to show that they have learned the new material, perhaps starting with the phrase: 'By the end of the lesson you should be able to...' This implies that you should also specify exactly what new ideas, knowledge or skills you want the pupils to learn as a result of the lesson.

Plan the method which you will use to enable the pupils to learn the material so that all the pupils can keep together as a class, everyone involved in the same activity for the same length of time, whether it be listening, answering questions orally or doing practice exercises.

Plan very specific ways of testing the pupils individually to assess how well they have learned what is intended. If possible, discuss your plan with the class teacher or college tutor to ensure that the lesson has the best possible chance of success.

Now, teach the lesson itself, noting particularly the following points:
(i) which pupils appear to learn the new material quickly and easily,
(ii) which pupils appear to have difficulty in understanding the material,
(iii) places in the lesson where, despite your plans, it is impossible to keep all the pupils together in their learning, so that you have to repeat, explain again, keep some pupils waiting while others catch up, etc.,
(iv) which pupils by the end of the lesson have learned what was intended and which have not fully succeeded.

Were the less successful learners among the ones whom you identified in the lesson itself? What sort of difficulties were encountered by the less successful, e.g. did they need more time? did they need explanations in simpler words?

did they need pictures, sketches, diagrams or familiar comparisons to help them to understand?

Using what you have learned about the pupils' performance, both as a group and as individuals in this lesson, plan a follow-up lesson building on the learning achieved, but making sure that those who had not fully understood all that was necessary have a chance to re-learn it, while those who were successful do not waste time on repetition. While it is not necessary for our immediate purpose it would be an advantage both to you and to the pupils to teach the follow-up lesson.

The previous exercise will have focused your attention on some individual differences which emerged during just one lesson, the principal ones being in the range of the levels of success in learning even when every pupil is apparently given the same classroom experience. Sometimes, it is true, it seems as though every pupil in the class has achieved the same level of learning by the end of the lesson but in almost every case this has been the result of the teacher giving additional explanations during the lesson to the pupils who need them, those who have already understood having to waste time while the rest catch up. In addition, every aware teacher knows that even when all pupils seem to have learned what is required by the end of the lesson itself, some will have forgotten important parts of it by the next lesson and will have to re-learn it.

What makes us different from everyone else?

Let us expand a little on some of the factors which contribute to making each individual different from every other person in the world. They will be dealt with here in very general terms which will be refined further during the course of the book, when additional reading will be recommended.

1 Factors with which one is born

When a baby is conceived by his parents he receives from each of them what is called genetic material which becomes part of the first and later cells which go to make up the body and all its parts. Conception happens when a sperm from the father enters and joins with an egg from the mother. The egg and sperm are very small and can be seen only under a very powerful microscope. The most important part of the sperm and egg is the *nucleus*, in each of which is a tangle of tiny string-like substances, called *chromosomes*. If one separated these and looked at them under a microscope one would see that there are twenty three chromosomes in both the egg and sperm, each one being made up of living material, called *genes*. When the male sperm enters the female egg each sperm chromosome pairs off with a similar one in the egg. This means that a fertilized egg, ready to develop into a new human being, has twenty three pairs of chromosomes, each made up of hundreds of genes, the whole thing being too small to be seen without a strong microscope. Small though they are, the genes carry what can be thought of as instructions to be followed by the new individual in its growth and development. Sometimes the instructions are very exact and the body has to obey them completely. At other times the instructions for development can be carried out more flexibly and, as we shall see, be influenced by things which happen outside the cells themselves. For example, the sex of the individual is decided at conception by one of the chromosomes which is contributed by the father. In about half the number of conceptions the father's sperm carries into the mother's egg a chromosome, called by biologists an 'X' chromosome, which is about the same length as all the rest of the twenty three. The mother's egg always has an 'X' chromosome in it. When both 'X' chromosomes are present the new cell is 'instructed' to grow into a female. In the other half of the conceptions, the father's sperm will carry into the mother's egg a shorter chromosome, called by the letter 'Y', which will 'instruct' the new cell to grow into a male. No matter what happens to the individual as he or she grows, there will be no choice but to become the sex which the genes, received at conception, decided.

Genes inherited from the parents decide many other physical traits. For example, the colour of one's skin and the structure of one's hair are determined by genetic inheritance, i.e. by the genes received from the parents at conception. There is very little that can be done to change the way in which the instructions are carried out. Of course, it is possible to change the inherited colour by dyeing or bleaching and hair can be straightened or curled. But once the treatment stops the hair or skin returns to its natural state. Certain diseases, such as the protein deficency disease of kwashiorkor, can make apparent changes to the skin and hair colour, black-skinned people becoming reddish-brown in colour. But the change is not permanent and once the poor diet is corrected the normal colour is restored.

An example of a more flexible genetically based trait is that of height. You have already noted the wide range of height difference among children in the same school class. You have probably noticed, too, that tallness or shortness tend to be typical of certain families. It is most likely that the genes one receives at conception decide how tall one would be able to grow if such factors as the quality of food, health, living conditions and so on throughout the person's growing years are the best possible. Very often, especially if at some stage the growing child was ill or badly fed, the greatest height that one's inheritance says could be reached is not in fact attained. We can never say for certain what the greatest possible height is in the case of any individual. The effect that disease, inadequate nutrition and living conditions can have on the development of children is illustrated by the poor growth and physical immaturity of many of those who are refugees from drought-stricken areas. It is very likely that, even if they eventually are able to live in good circumstances, free of disease and receiving an adequate and well-balanced diet, they will always be smaller than their genes would be expected to allow. It is probable, too, that their full learning capacity will not be reached because of their experiences. Even when there is reasonable nutrition and good living conditions, there is evidence that genetic potential (i.e. what one's inheritance would allow one to achieve if all circumstances were ideal) is not always fully reached, at least as far as height is concerned. In both industrialized countries, and among, for example, the Zimbabwean boarding school population, children of the present generation are on the average taller than their grandparents were at the same age, probably the result of healthier living conditions and a greater understanding of the diet needs for sound growth.

Inheritance through the genes is also thought to contribute to the individual differences that you have already noticed in pupils' abilities to learn in school. Note that I have used the words 'contributed to' instead of 'are responsible for'. There are important differences in the meaning of these two phrases. The first one implies that only part of the individual differences can be accounted for by genetic inheritance and the second one suggests that the individual differences are entirely caused by inheritance.

As we shall see later, there is plenty of evidence to suggest that our genes determine the learning ability which we *could* develop, i.e. our learning *potential*, if we have the right chances. Whether we actually reach our full potential depends on many non-genetic factors. All children have different home and school experiences, i.e. they all have different *environments*. It appears that some environments help or hold back the development of some aspects of learning. We shall see later that children who, from the earliest years, have the opportunity to explore and find out things for themselves and who spend plenty of time with older people and thus learn to use language competently and share ideas with them, seem to develop their learning ability to a greater extent than do children who have had less experience of these things. There are many other factors which will be mentioned later. At this moment, it is enough for you to know that there is strong evidence to suggest that the individual differences in learning ability stem in part from inheritance, very considerably modified by a wide range of personal circumstances, some of which can be changed by parents and teachers.

To summarise the immediate position, it could be said that, while it is important to recognise that the differences in learning ability are very real and must be taken into account in one's teaching, there is a strong possibility that every pupil's capacity to learn could be improved, within his own personal limits, by a teacher who uses methods which will enable him to learn *how* to learn and how to use his intellectual capacities to the full. In general, teaching methods which require a pupil to ask questions and to find the answers for themselves and to extend their experience, either directly or through books and pictures, to solve problems and to undertake many other intellectual activities, will be more successful as far as the pupil is concerned. Such methods will also help them to make fuller use of the intellectual capacities that they have, than will teaching methods which merely require pupils to remember collections of facts which are presented to them. In the same way, teaching methods which make allowances for individual learning capacities will be generally more successful than those which expect each pupil to do exactly the same work, in the same way and time as every other pupil in the class.

In addition to our general ability to learn, it seems likely that some special mental abilities may be influenced partly by our genetic inheritance and partly by the experiences and opportunities that our home and school environments give us. For example, some people seem to be more able then others to develop their thinking abilities through words and language, i.e. their verbal skills, while others seem to be happier handling ideas which involve numbers, shapes, spaces, diagrams, maps and other non-verbal ways of thinking. Some people are much more able than others to use their imaginations and think up new ways of doing things, i.e. thinking creatively. Others are more comfortable dealing with real and practical situations. We shall examine at a later stage and in greater detail the importance of these for the teacher in the classroom. As with general intellectual (learning) capacity, there is evidence that suggests that, while there is probably a genetic factor which sets the possible limits for these abilities, educational and other environmental experiences are important in deciding how far each person's ability is developed for use. This means that individual differences cannot be wiped out, no matter what methods we use. On the other hand well-selected educational methods and learning opportunities can increase almost everyone's ability and skill in any of the above mental areas, allowing the genetic 'instructions' to be carried out more completely.

Considerable responsibility, therefore, rests with the teacher, not merely to ensure that his pupils cover the content of the syllabus but also that in doing so, he uses teaching methods and learning activities which will give the pupils opportunities to develop their thinking skills. Such skills are part of every country's wealth and must not be wasted by being underdeveloped. This is especially important among communities that have had a relatively late start in determining their own affairs and becoming self-sufficient in the twentieth century world.

In addition to the more obvious intellectual ones, some individual differences in personality habits seem to have a genetic basis, though much influenced by actual experiences and upbringing. Think back to the classes you have taught or are teaching, and to classes and student groups of which you have been a member. Every member of such groups has his own characteristic way of behaving and reacting, and his learning success is often much influenced by this. There is, for example, the overconfident person and the one who rushes at a task without first being sure that he knows exactly what is required of him. Then there is the rather fearful person who is not confident enough to ask for help. The daydreamer is often apparently not aware of what is going on around him, while the person who can comfortably grasp large and complex ideas may find that working steadily at day-to-day detailed tasks bores him so much that he avoids them as much as possible, sometimes doing himself harm educationally. And what about the person who always makes the least possible effort in any task? You can, I am sure, think of many more personality traits which can influence approaches to learning in schools and achievement.

The teacher cannot change a person's basic personality and should not try to do so. But he can help his pupils to develop study habits which will reduce the effect of those personal characteristics which prevent them from benefitting fully from their school opportunities. This means that the teacher must get to know his pupils as individual people as soon and as well as possible and, within the limits of the school situation, help each to understand himself and how he can make the most of his good qualities and reduce the worst effects of the less useful ones. The formal education system, as well as the home and the wider community, has a contribution to make to the development of mature, healthy personalities who can become effective and responsible members of the adult world. No society wants only one type of personality but in every society there are certain character traits and behaviours which are more acceptable than others, and these vary from group to group. The school plays an important part in helping young people to fit into their own environments, emphasising the important qualities and helping to control the unacceptable ones. This can best be achieved by teachers who, firstly, understand the uniqueness of each pupil in their care (the result of interaction between the potential with which they are born and previous experience) and secondly, are sensitive to the personal qualities valued by the culture of which their pupils are a part. These points will be dealt with at greater depth and practicality later in the book. At this point, it is enough to create awarenecss of your responsibility, in the hope that you will be more conscious than before of the individuality of each of your pupils and of some of the factors which can help him develop satisfactorily within his own limits.

2 Factors from outside oneself

In the first part of this chapter you were introduced to the idea that how well an individual develops and learns is partly decided by the genes that he receives from his parents when he is conceived. The genes, however, can only decide what *could* happen *if* all the circumstances were ideal. Every individual has lived since birth in his own personal environment, with experiences and opportunities different from every other individual's. These experiences help to decide how his inherited potential will develop. Some environmental influences seem to increase the differences between individuals, making it difficult for them to be grouped together and to be expected to do the same things in the same way. Other influences, fortunately for teachers, seem to reduce some individual differences, making it possible to arrange pupils in groups and classes of children who have enough similarities for them to be taught together. For convenience, we call the range of individual differences within a group its 'variability'.

a) Factors which tend to reduce the variability within a group
These relate firstly to the extent to which members of the group come from similar home backgrounds. Included in this similarity are such things as the parents' own educational levels, the sort of work they do, the money they earn and what they expect the school to do for their children. Also included are similarities of culture and ethnic origin. Individual differences will still exist but the teacher's task will be eased a little when trying to cater for his pupils' needs. Secondly, variability within a group can be reduced by the school, if it arranges pupils into classes or groups in such a way that the range of differences is reduced. Thirdly, teachers can, and often do, reduce the range of individual differences by treating a group or class as though it was made up of nearly identical people, at least as far as their capacity for school learning is concerned. It would be useful to refer back to the observations which you made in Application 4, in which you were asked to watch a lesson, noting occasions when the teacher seemed to treat all pupils in the same way. Research shows that, for example, when children are consistently taught by a teacher who tells them all the facts, giving them little opportunity to think, find out for themselves and use their imaginations creatively, even the naturally creative pupils lose some of their ability to think creatively, thus reducing the range of ability differences. The opposite situation, that of offering extensive opportunities to think creatively and imaginatively will have the effect of widening the group differences in this area, since those with more natural creative ability than others will develop their potential more fully while those with only average endowment will make some progress, but not as much as the above average.

The same applies to other aspects of intellectual ability, commonly called *intelligence*. There is plenty of evidence to suggest that some aspects of one's inborn potential can remain underdeveloped in an educational and cultural environment which does not require the child to solve problems for himself or follow through his own thinking with some independence of the teacher or other adults. Individual differences within such a situation would be reduced because even those with high intellectual potential could remain unstretched. Sameness within any class or group can be encouraged by education systems which value the learning of collections of facts rather than the ability to use factual knowledge to develop one's own ideas and thinking ability. It can also be encouraged by individual teachers, especially those who undervalue individual differences and underestimate the influence that a teacher can have on the development of potential abilities in their pupils.

b) Factors which tend to encourage the variability within a group
These factors, as one would expect, are those which are not common to the whole school, community or class and are usually related to the individual's family and home. For example, some children have parents who spend a lot of time with them, talking to them, answering questions and helping them to find their own answers, reading books to them and providing them with books to read for themselves. Such parents often take their children to see things of interest in their own districts or even in their own homes and gardens. By contrast, there are many other parents who, although they have no less money or education than the ones just described, give very little personal attention of the kind mentioned. They are not cruel, or deliberately neglectful but, for a variety of reasons they do not consider that they should provide the intellectual stimulation that the first type of parent does. Such personal circumstances can increase individual differences because they can affect school performance, not only in the store of factual knowledge that the child brings to the school with him but also in his ability to express himself in words, in his motivation and his general interest in learning in school. Children from interested and stimulating homes are likely to be more successful learners in school than are those from the other type described.

The sort of experiences that children from extended and traditional families have are likely to be very different from those of children from what are known as 'nuclear families' (i.e. those which consist of father, mother and their own children). In the former, the child is involved with many adults, most of whom have a recognised part to play in his upbringing. He may also be one of a large number of children, some of whom are his own brothers and sisters but others the children of his parents' relatives living as part of the extended family. He is likely to have mixed with and been looked after by older children from a fairly early age; he is also likely to have had to take some responsibility for younger children as he grows older. Thus he will have had less personal involvement with adults despite the number who surround him. On the other hand, a child from a nuclear family, whose parents are directly responsible for his upbringing, are likely to have had closer interaction with adults than a child from an extended family. Such differences in the sort of contact that children have had with the adults in their lives are likely to increase the range of individual differences within a group.

As well as the differences from family to family in attitudes towards the upbringing of their children, there are more general group differences which it is important to consider. Your attention was drawn in Application 6, especially in questions 7 and 10, to those which relate to the home language of the pupils, which may differ from that which is used in the school, and to the education and employment of the parents. There is evidence that suggests that school progress can be influenced by such things as these. Then, too, many countries and districts are multi-cultural or multi-ethnic, each group having its own customs and expectations of their children, which can increase other environmental differences. For example, many African peoples, of whom Kpelle parents in Liberia are typical, consider that it is not the place of children to ask questions of adults. It is thought to be disrespectful towards them. Children brought up in this way are likely to continue to be reluctant to ask questions of the teacher, being content to accept his authority and to be told what to do rather than to think for themselves. Traditionally the Kipsigis of Kenya encourage children to be silent in the presence of adults. Recently, an increasing number of Kipsigis mothers, possibly because many of them have been to school, are encouraging their children, from an early age, to talk more freely in the presence of adults. Children of such mothers are noticeably readier to ask questions and to make their own decisions.

A final example of a family and cultural expectation which may affect the way in which children react in school, concerns some nursery school children which the author was observing. They were urban African children aged between 4 and 6 years who attended a nursery school in a town in Zimbabwe. One of the hardest tasks that the teachers met was to persuade the children to move about freely. Instead, they were quite content to sit on benches and wait for the teacher to talk to them. At first the reason could have been lack of confidence in an unfamiliar situation, or the presence of an observer. But the behaviour continued for many months, only gradually allowing spontaneity to develop. Compared with Western children of the same age they were very 'well-behaved'. It must be added that these observations were made twenty years ago, when nursery schooling was in its infancy. Recent observations of similar children in the same school showed that a change was taking place. Teachers are now commenting that their young pupils are much 'naughtier' than they used to be, by which they mean that they are less likely to sit still, accept suggestions as to what to do and generally treat adults with deference. It is probably significant that these children are at least second generation urban, their parents having also been born and brought up in a town, whereas their grandparents most likely lived much of their earlier years in rural areas.

Some cultures consider it a breach of good manners for individuals to excel in competition with each other, so that rivalry between individuals or groups cannot be used to motivate children to learn. Instead, some form of personal challenge and a technique which will help each pupil to monitor his own progress may have to be adopted by the teacher. In other cultures, it is not thought proper for girls to compete with boys, especially if they do better than the boys. The result is that girls may tend to do less than their best when in a mixed sex class, i.e. a co-educational class, only the very strong minded being bold enough to ignore such a custom.

This point was brought home to the author when visiting a co-educational academic secondary school in a town in Zimbabwe. At that time there was rigorous selection for the relatively few available school places so that it was reasonable to assume that all the pupils, both boys and girls, were of high scholastic achievement. By chance one of the two parallel classes observed consisted mostly of boys, with only three or four girls. The other class had a majority of girls in it. Both classes were taught the same syllabuses by the same teachers. It was noticeable that in the first class the girls remained very quiet, rarely volunteering an answer or asking a question. When they did they seemed very unsure of themselves. Some of the teachers tended to ignore the girls which probably reinforced the limited part that they played in class. By contrast, in the second class the girls were lively, confident and ready to show that they were as competent as the boys while not being afraid to make a mistake. The boys, it must be said, did not remain quietly in the background but did their best to make sure that they were not outdone by the girls.

A further problem, more common in developing than in

developed countries, is an attitude which sees girls either as less important educationally or as less able than boys to learn in school. Such attitudes often result in serious underachievement by girls and a reluctance on the part of parents and even the girls themselves, to use the avaliable educational opportunities to the full. Thus the range of intellectual and educational development among children is increased.

The list of environmental circumstances which can influence the educational achievement and needs of individuals and groups is endless. The main point for you as a teacher, at present, is that you must at all times be conscious of the fact that each of your pupils brings with him into the classroom the results of many personal, family and environmental influences which can affect his about the backgrounds of the major groups in your class, the general social and economic setting of the districts from which most of your pupils are drawn, the sorts of experiences that their homes and neighbourhoods have provided and the commoner attitudes of parents towards their children and what they expect them to get from their schooling. You may not be able to make provision for each of your pupils individually, but you should be able to cater for the needs of most of them because you now have a realistic foundation to build your teaching programme on.

There is research that suggests that, since teachers as a group, especially in Third World countries, tend to come from homes which valued education for their children and gave them every chance to complete their schooling, they may, without realising it, handicap some of their pupils whose own home backgrounds are less than favourable. They may, for example, be unaware of the difficulties that some of their pupils may have at home. Such conditions as serious overcrowding, poor lighting, very few toys or books, no quiet place where older children can do their homework, heavy domestic responsibilities, especially for girls, are still widespread. As the provision of schooling expands and attendance becomes compulsory, the numbers of children from educationally unfavourable homes must also increase. It is important that teachers make a conscious effort to think of their pupils in their *real* home and community setting. School and teachers must beome part of the pupil's total environment, making allowances and compensating for any unfavourable features. This point will be enlarged upon in a later chapter.

Finally, in rapidly developing and multi-cultural countries there is a wide range of quality of school provision and of geographical, cultural and home environments. Teachers may find themselves in schools and districts very different from those with which they are familar. It is particularly important that in such circumstances teachers get to know and, to some extent, become part of the new surroundings in order to understand their pupils and their learning needs.

Application 8

The photographs on pages 35 and 36 show contrasting environments commonly found in developing or Third World countries. They show a typical African village scene, a scene from a working class suburb and a middle class suburb in a modern African city.

For *at least one* of the pictures, preferably the one which will be closest to the sort of district in which you expect to teach, find answers to the following questions, checking them wherever possible from your own observation.

1 What schooling have most of the adults had?
2 What do most parents hope that the school will do for their children?
3 What language do most children speak at home? Is it different from the major one used in their school?
4 Do the parents feel that education is more important for boys than girls? Or do they think that boys and girls should learn different things in school?
5 Are the families mostly 'extended', i.e. consist not only of parents and children but also of other relatives living in a close group, often sharing the responsibility for the children's care and upbringing? Or are most families 'nuclear', consisting of father, mother and their children? Are there many 'polygamous' families, i.e. the father having more than one wife?
6 How many rooms (or huts) does the family have to live in and approximately how many family members would there be to each room? Is there usually reasonable space for children to do set homework or private study?
7 What form of lighting and heating is there, wood, paraffin, candles, electricity, etc.?
8 Are there likely to be books, newspapers or other reading material in the homes? Are there libraries in the district and can children borrow books? How many children do borrow books fairly regularly?
9 What sort of play materials do most children have at home, e.g. traditional ones made from local materials, simple shop-bought ones, technically complex and expensive ones?
10 What games do children mostly play, perhaps at different ages, and girls differently from boys?

11 What tools and mechanical equipment are the children likely to be familiar with, e.g. traditional hoes, hand or ox-drawn ploughs, traditional clay pots for carrying water, ox-drawn sledges or wheeled carts, bicycles, sewing machines, piped water, wind or motor pumps for water and irrigation, motor cars, buses, trains, radios, televisions, refrigerators, electric stoves, etc.
12 How many children have visited local places of interest, such as game parks, dams, lakes, factories, supermarkets, museums, etc.?
13 How likely is it that many children will have travelled more than ten miles from their own home district. If so, from where?
14 What medical facilities are easily available to them, e.g. district nurses, occasional or regular clinics, hospitals, private doctors etc.?

There are a great many more questions which could usefully be asked about children and their backgrounds and it is hoped that you will add them to your list when they occur to you. Discuss your results with fellow students, especially those who studied a different environment. At this stage what use do you think you could make of the information if you were a teacher?

1   *A typical village scene*

2   An overcrowded urban scene

3   A middle class city suburb

Further reading

Wagner, D.A. and Stevenson, H.W., (eds.), *Cultural Perspectives on Child Development*; San Francisco, W.H. Freeman and Co., 1982. Read especially Chapter 9, pp.181 to 207. You would find it interesting to read the whole book, though perhaps not all at once.

Thompson, A.R. *Education and Development in Africa*, London, Macmillan, 1981, especially Chapter 10, pp 262 to 306.

CHAPTER FOUR

Common Trends in development and learning

Despite the fact that teachers have a duty to develop each individual pupil to his fullest extent, schools and education systems as they are usually organized make it necessary for teachers to be able to identify and use the many similarities which exist, as well as to be able to allow for personal variations. The realities of most education systems make it necessary to organize pupils into groups of varying size and composition for many learning experiences. In addition to this, the nature of human beings and human society is such that people need to understand and make the best use of their similarities to others as well as to develop their individuality. People need to be individuals within the groups to which they belong, but not to the extent that they have little in common with their fellows. In turn, the society which provides the education system expects it to produce people who not only have the knowledge and skills that it requires but who also accept its rules and values. It is more concerned with its own preservation, development and ability to function than with developing individuality for its own sake. The teacher's task is to find a balance between the individual and the group, planning his teaching so that each pupil has his own personal chance to achieve the common educational purpose, which must include not merely covering the items listed in the syllabus but developing qualities such as those which his family, community and the wider society require their members to have.

Fortunately for teachers and those who have to deal with large numbers of people, human development generally follows an almost universal pattern, in that the order in which progress is made is much the same for everyone. It seems that those inherited 'instructions' included in the genes which are responsible for the gradual unfolding of capacities are the same for all normal human beings, in a pattern or order which crosses ethnic and cultural barriers. For example, any normal child, anywhere in the world, whose central nervous system has matured enough in response to inherited instructions to enable him to identify and reproduce sounds which he hears, will begin to learn to speak intelligibly. Linguists have identified a more or less universal pattern by which children analyse what they hear, identify and use the rules of grammar and develop their own vocabularies until they are able to communicate complex and abstract ideas through the use of spoken language. This can become a written language as well, should the necessary learning opportunities occur. Of course, the actual language spoken will be that of the people among whom the child lives, and the age and rate at which the language will be learned and used will vary from individual to individual, depending both on his inborn learning capacities and the learning opportunities offered by his own environment.

Similarly, in the development of physical capacities there is an almost universal pattern of growth spurts followed by periods of slower consolidation until adulthood, sexual maturity being completed within the second ten years of life. This last point is a good illustration of the variation within the universal order. It is easy to see, for example, the age at which a boy's voice 'breaks', one of the signs of approaching sexual and physical maturity. Within any group there can be as much as four years age range within which the voice change will normally happen. But investigation will show that in an age group of adolescent boys in the same school and from fairly common backgrounds, up to three-quarters of them will have voices which 'break' within a year of each other. A small number will experience an early voice break while an almost similar number will experience a late one. Most will group round the centre point of the age range. The actual age at which the breaking happens will depend to some extent on the genetic inheritance of the individual but it will also depend upon certain environmental factors, especially those related to nutrition, disease patterns, habits of rest and exercise and so on. In Western industrialised countries where the nutrition and health of children have improved greatly during this century, the average age of *puberty* (the term for the attainment of sexual maturity) is now several years earlier than it was. But the developmental sequence is maintained as well as the individual differences.

As we shall see later, there is thought to be a universal order in which thinking and reasoning capacities develop, children being unable to use forms of logic and reasoning which have not yet matured. Here again, it is impossible to separate the inherited potential from the influence of the environment and the opportunities they may have to learn how to think. On the other hand, if teachers have some knowledge of what pattern of development to expect and how to identify the point in the progression at which an individual or a group is likely to be, they have a reasonable chance of planning learning activities which will build on the existing abilities and thus make the most of the available potential.

It is a common educational practice to classify learners in some way so that they can be managed by teachers in classes, groups or forms. Before going into details you will need to undertake more observational tasks.

Application 9

Arrange to spend enough time in at least one primary and one secondary school to enable you to answer the following questions and to discuss the reasons behind the answers with the Head and/or staff members of the school.

1. On what basis are the classes or forms within the school organized, e.g. are the children divided into classrooms according to:
   chronological age (i.e. their real age),
   sex,
   school attainment as shown in test and examination results,
   random selection (i.e. on no regular basis),
   previous school experience,
   home language?
   There may well be other criteria for selection (i.e. bases for inclusion) not listed above, or there may be combinations of more than one.
2. Discuss with the Head and/or teachers in the school the reasons for the criteria of selection used in allocating children to their classes, forms or groups and what they see to be the advantages and disadvantages of the structure. If, as sometimes happens, the criteria are decided by outside bodies such as the local education committee or a board of governors, discuss with the Head and others what criteria they would prefer, given the choice, and why.
3. For as many classes or forms as possible in each school, with a minimum of two in each, find out the basis on which the teacher

makes sub-groups within his or her class, possibly for some but not all learning situations. These could include such criteria as:
- sex, in that boys and girls may be expected to take different subjects,
- attainment in the subject matter,
- age and apparent ability in classes where there is a wide age range,
- personal interests of the pupils,
- friendship groups,
- random groups, etc..

If there are no formal groups within the class either on a regular or occasional basis, make a note of this and try to find out how the teacher deals with individual differences in attainment and needs.

4 Discuss with each teacher his or her reasons for the criteria which they use, their strengths and limitations and what improvements could be made if necessary.

Note If you are an employed teacher you should still undertake this task both in your own school and elsewhere and add notes about your own practices and your justification for them. If at all possible, discuss your findings with colleagues and fellow students.

The criteria used for selecting or grouping learners are usually chosen because they fit in with what those who are responsible believe to be factors which reduce individual differences. One of the most obvious is chronological age, teachers *assuming* (or believing) that children who are near each other in age will be sufficiently similar in developmental levels and needs for them to be manageable in a group. It is a useful exercise for you to try to identify some of the assumptions (or beliefs) about development and learning that underly the main criteria for selection and grouping. Your study of psychology should help you to decide whether or not the beliefs are justified or whether there are better ways of handling individual differences.

Application 10

Here is a list of the more common criteria by which groups are formed. For each one write down briefly what assumptions are implied about how children develop and learn. For example, if the order of marks received in a test are used with the top thirty five children being put together in one class, the assumption is that the test results are an indication of how well the pupils would be able to learn in future. There is also the assumption that the test actually measured, accurately and widely, their knowledge and understanding of the subject matter. As we shall see later this is not always the case.

When you have recorded your own ideas of the assumptions underlying each criterion, read to the end of this chapter and compare your ideas with those given. Are you now better able to do this task?

Criteria
chronological age
sex
school attainment based on test and examination results
previous teacher's recommendations
parents' requests
standardized attainment tests (i.e. those intended for use by many schools)
standardized intelligence tests (i.e. test which try to measure the quality of a person's mental capacity rather than what he has learned)
home language
religious beliefs
random (e.g. according to the initial letter of the surname, day pupils only or boarding pupils only)
previous school experience
attainment in one or two selected school subjects e.g. reading ability, scientific and mathematical attainment, etc..
If you have found any other criteria in your own investigations, include them in your analysis.

Probably the most common basis on which the allocation of school pupils to classes or forms is made, is that of chronological age. It is a very convenient criterion and is based on the assumption that most children, at least from a fairly common background, go through the developmental stages in more or less the same order and attain the same level at about the same time. There is indeed some truth in this assumption, but only in very general terms. In Application 6 (paragraph 4) you observed some of the variation in only one aspect of development, that of physical height. The majority of children of the same age were grouped about the same height, but several were noticeably taller than this average and several others were noticeably shorter. There are many other aspects of development which are less easily observed and accurately measured than physical height but much more important for teaching and learning. They include intellectual and personality factors which are also thought to unfold and mature in a regular order, to some extent in relation to chronological age. As with height, these factors develop more quickly in some people than in others, with most crowding around the middle point. Some of the more important of these for the teacher will be dealt with in more detail later.

At present it is enough to accept that, while chronological age is a common and convenient basis on which to group children, care must be taken not to assume that they have all, or even nearly all, reached the same place on the development pattern. It does, however, give the teacher a rough guide for the purposes of comparing actual developmental levels with those described in books on developmental psychology. It is worth noticing that as children become older, the range of developmental differences within an age group widens and chronological age becomes a less useful basis for education selection and classification.

A second common basis for selection into classes and forms is the level of achievement that was shown by individuals in previous schools or classes. The usual practice is to try to keep children together who are more or less the same age, grouping them into classes according to how well they have learned in the past. This is commonly known as 'streaming', probably bacause each group is expected to flow like a stream along its own course at its own pace, without there being too many obstacles to its progress. Obstacles in this sense would be individual pupils who find the general pace of the stream too slow, or who cannot keep up with the rest. Just as real streams differ as to their speed of flow and to the width and depth of their course, so, it is hoped, can streamed classes.

'Streaming' also makes several educational and developmental assumptions about children and learning. Firstly, it assumes that because someone has shown a certain level of learning in the past he will continue to show that level in the future. If he has found learning easy and made excellent progress he is expected to continue to do so. If, on the other hand he has found learning difficult in the past, he is expected to continue to do so, even if the subject matter and teaching approaches change. It takes no account of the possibility that some, who have until now progressed rapidly and in advance of the others, may experience a levelling off of their maturity rate. In the same way, it does not take into account the possibility of others who were slower to start finding their maturity rate speeding up later on. There is also the possibility that teachers will assume that the range of individual differences and needs in a streamed class are so slight that they are tempted to ignore them.

The use of marks, reports and previous recommendations as bases on which to stream pupils makes assumptions that these reflect the real ability and attainment of the pupils. As we shall see later (Chapter Twelve) this is rarely the case, so that it is important that teachers of children in streamed classes keep an open mind about their pupils and their abilities, and avoid placing too much reliance on other people's assessments.

In countries where there is still a shortage of school places at secondary school level, the authorities face the problem of having to make sure that those most likely to benefit from further schooling are identified. An increasing number make selection procedures fairer by setting tests and examinations that all children of the right age group sit. This does away with the need to use school marks and reports and provides a common basis on which selection can be made. One can appreciate the necessity for such procedures until the need for them drops away, but it is still important to bear in mind the assumptions about children that such methods make. They assume that the tests set and the marks gained are good indicators of an individual's future performance. They also assume that those who do not score highly enough will not benefit from further educational opportunity, whereas those who score highly will.

Experience in many countries shows that, too often, children who are selected in this way are not as able as expected. The author experienced the reverse situation some years ago in pre-independence Zimbabwe. At that time there was about one secondary school place for every twenty African primary school leavers. Selection was on the results of what was known as the Grade Seven examination, taken in the last year of primary school. A voluntary group of which the author was a member, was concerned that so many young people who were obviously capable of going further educationally should be turned away, without even much chance of employment because they were young. A voluntary school was started, with very few resources and inadequate premises. Most of the teachers were volunteers and most of the books and equipment were donated. While the aim of the school was to provide a good basic education rather than to enable the pupils to gain academic certificates, they were allowed to enter for the Government Junior Certificate examination (external) in subjects such as Ndebele, English, Arithmetic, Biology, Typing, etc.. Even though these first pupils had only five terms of secondary school in contrast to the six terms that their former school mates who were admitted to an official secondary school had, their examination results were, on the whole, even better than those of the latter children. They got higher grades overall on all the subjects for which they entered. This is not the place to speculate why this was ... motivation? smaller classes? more dedicated teachers? etc.. But the point is made that teachers and education authorities must be cautious when assuming that examinations, marks etc. are in themselves good predictors of success or failure at subsequent levels.

In summary, then, it seems that many educational practices are based on assumptions about the nature of children and how they develop and learn. The chief assumptions are firstly, that despite all the visible and invisible differences among children there is, nevertheless, a pattern of development which is common enough to enable children within a fairly narrow age band to be taught more or less the same things at about the same age, especially if one makes sub-groups based on apparent ability and achievement. The second major assumption is that it is possible to assess the apparent ability and achievement by the use of tests, reports and observations and thus predict to some extent what to expect in the future. We shall look more closely at the truth or otherwise about these assumptions later in the book and make proposals for teachers. In the meantime, it is important that you develop the habit of asking questions about educational practices that are widely taken for granted. In this way you will come to know more about your pupils and bring to your teaching a freshness of approach which will be good both for you and for them. It is very likely that you will in some instances decide that the hidden assumptions are in fact sound and the way in which they have been interpreted, in educational terms, justified. But that does not in any way reduce the value of questioning them in the first place.

To return to the starting point of this chapter, that there is a common pattern of development which all normal human beings follow. It must be obvious by now that if teachers are to plan for successful learning by their pupils they must become familiar with features of the developmental pattern at which their pupils are likely to be. This familiarity must include a knowledge of the most obvious signs which can give a clue to the development level actually achieved and what direction the next natural step is likely to take. This must be done, not only in order to make it possible for them to plan immediate learning activities for their pupils, but also to enable them to prepare the ground for further developmental progress by the pupils. Research evidence suggests, as has already been said, that development is an interactive process between inherited possibilities and environmental opportunities. Without the latter, the former may not able to exert its full influence. It is not as easy as it may sound for a teacher to obtain an immediately usable understanding of the important aspects of the developmental expectations for his pupils. Most textbooks deal either with the pattern throughout the life-span in such general terms that a teacher would find it virtually impossible to make use of the information in his teaching; or it may be in such detail that he would need to be a professional psychologist to be able to select and use the relevant aspects. A factor complicating the problem in a professional course for intending teachers is that most students are preparing to teach within a fairly limited age and/or ability range of pupils. It is a rare education system which uses its teachers so flexibly that they can expect to teach at any level from pre-school to upper secondary. While it is very important for teachers of any age group to have a general idea of what the developmental processes of their pupils have been up to the present and what they can be expected to be in the future, what is really needed is a more detailed knowledge of the range of pupils whom they expect to teach. A book such as this, which, it is hoped, will be of help to teachers at all levels of education, cannot give more than a general description of the normal developmental pattern. The student or teacher must seek more detailed information elsewhere, and also constantly observe his pupils closely to build up from his own experience, as true a picture as possible of his pupils.

A further difficulty lies in the fact that there are different facets of development, some apparently more important to the teacher than others. The most common relate to:

a) *physical growth and development*, which includes not only growth in body size but the development of capacities for increasingly complex movements and physical activities involving muscles, the central and peripheral (i.e. extended) nervous systems, etc.;

b) *intellectual growth and development*, which includes not merely the capacity to absorb more information but to use increasingly specialised and complex thinking and reasoning processes;

c) *social development*, which includes the development of the capacity to act properly in increasingly complicated social settings, so that ultimately the individual is able to feel confident and comfortable in most of the situations that he meets;

d) *emotional development*, which includes an increasing ability to control and channel one's feelings and reactions so that one can fit in comfortably with one's family, friends, neighbours and fellow citizens.

As you will see, none of these aspects of development takes place on its own; each one is always influenced in some way by the others. But we must focus on each separately in order to understand the developmental processes and to make suitable provisions for them. For example, if intellectual development is proceeding normally but social and emotional development are handicapped by home or school circumstances, a child may not be able to make full use of the ability that he has because his attention and energy are diverted to his personal concerns. His attitudes to success and failure and his ability to work co-operatively with others, or independently, may be so far out of step with the rest of his development, and with that of his age group as a whole, that his achievement is seriously reduced. Similarly the child's physical state, health, nutrition and size in relation to the rest of the group may prevent him from gaining full benefit from his schooling. As you will see later, there is a close relationship between the level of an individual's intellectual development and the sort of decisions he makes about how to behave; these in turn are influenced by his social and emotional development.

In the light of all these difficulties, then, how best can a teacher gain the necessary understanding of the developmental processes and needs of his pupils in order to teach successfully? In the next chapter, there will be an outline of some of the more important general processes with some indication of average ages at which they may occur and some of the factors which seem to influence them. But such information is only a starting point. In addition, you should read in more detail from other texts, of which some references will be given at the end of the chapter, about the development of young people within the age range that you are likely to teach. Above all, it will be necessary over the years for you to observe your pupils realistically, asking yourself questions about the extent to which the group as a whole and individuals within it fit your ideas of what their capacities are. A constantly questioning and flexible attitude will help you to benefit from your growing experience which will, in turn, make your teaching more successful and rewarding. It will also enable you to keep in touch with your pupils as the gap between your generation and theirs grows. This is especially important in rapidly changing countries. Young people in ten years time are likely to be different from those whom you meet today. In Third World countries there are already likely to be wide differences between groups from rural and urban backgrounds, or between groups from different cultural or ethnic backgrounds, so that a flexible and questioning attitude is particularly necessary.

You can see that a foundation of knowledge about the general principles of the developmental process, a wider and more detailed study of the ages with which you are personally involved and a sensitive but humble attitude to the breadth of one's own knowledge are the essentials for successful educators at any level.

Further reading

Wagner, D.A. and Stevenson, H.W., (eds.); *Cultural Perspectives on Child Development*, San Francisco, W.H. Freeman and Co., 1982, pp 54-76.

Since you need to know as much as possible about the children whom you expect to teach, you should ask in your own library and any others accessible to you, for books and articles which deal with children in your own country. The Education and Psychology Departments in universities, research articles from medical schools, etc., are good sources of local information on child development and the special circumstances that may affect it.

CHAPTER FIVE

The developing child

This chapter aims at giving you a very general picture of the major features of the growing child. It will illustrate the orderliness and the universal nature of human development but it can serve only as a starting point from which to make your educational plans and decisions and cannot be used as a model of what you can expect of each child that you meet. In line with common educational practice, chronological ages have been used as the major criteria for the groups described, average ages at which the signs of development occur being the ones on which the descriptions are based. All the various influences which contribute to individual differences in development must be taken into account as well in order to fill out the picture of any child or groups of children actually in front of you. Later in the chapter, activities will be suggested which should help you to turn the general pictures into more detailed ones for your own use. When reading and thinking about this chapter don't yield to the temptation of skipping over those age groups with which you are not directly concerned. There are good reasons for this, including the fact that all children can only be understood in the light of their previous development and experience. They also need to be put onto the road which leads to the next stage of normal development. Then, too, there is much individual difference in the rate at which individuals pass along the continuum (i.e. the orderly progress of development) so that some could be at a level normally expected of older or younger children.

The child from eighteen months to six years

This is an important period during which the child has much to learn, and indeed actually learns a great deal, about the world in which he finds himself and about the people in it. He begins the stage as a fairly dependent individual, usually able to walk and run, though often unsteadily and in an unco-ordinated way. He is likely to be clumsy with his hands and unable to make fine movements with his fingers. He will understand some words and use a few of them, the structure of his sentences being very simple. He will enjoy, and need to be with, people he knows but he is not able to play co-operatively with others. His span of attention will be short and he soon becomes annoyed if frustrated. His great strengths are his enormous motivation to learn, his curiosity and his desire for independence. His major developmental needs are opportunities to experience widely, to practise both physical and social skills and to develop his language, both as a way of understanding and dealing with his physical world and of developing good relationships with others. Above all, he needs a secure, loving family within which he can reach out with confidence to the larger world and develop his maturing potential to the full.

4   Five year olds learning through play

By the time he is ready to enter formal school, at about the age of six, he has a great deal of control over his body and its muscles, and can run, climb and jump skilfully and confidently. He can use the finer muscles of his hands to pick up and use a pencil and simple tools co-ordinating the movements with those of his eyes with fair competence. He also has acquired considerable physical independence.

During this period he will extend his social competence and confidence so that he will be able to accept separation from his parents, and other people whom he knows well, for a few hours at a time, though he will still need the secure base of his familiar home. He will have learned to co-operate with others, to share both material things and the attention of adults and will be able to work and play with other children in genuine interaction rather than the earlier phase in which he liked to play in the company of others while being occupied with his own games. By the age of six, most children will be able to control most of their aggressive urges and be able to concentrate for longer periods (ten or fifteen minutes) on one activity, and to listen with interest to stories. In most, but not all societies and cultures, children will be able, by this age, to recognise themselves as either boys or girls and there is an increasing tendency for children to choose to play with others of the same sex and even with toys which are thought of as appropriate for their sex.

Intellectually, most children will have made great strides by the time they reach six. They will have acquired an extensive and complex language and be able to use it freely, even creatively. They will be capable of bringing enthusiasm and energy to most learning tasks and be anxious to acquire the skills and knowledge that older children and adults have. Through the previous years they will have made considerable progress in being able to understand their world and how many things in it work. There is, however, evidence to suggest that they still learn and understand their world in direct and practical ways rather than as abstract ideas and they can think about only one aspect of it at a time, rather than several different aspects interacting with one another. This will be dealt with in more detail when discussing intellectual development; for the moment it is enough to accept that despite the great distance that they have come, intellectually, since babyhood, six-year-olds still need much direct first-hand experience and practice in their real and solid worlds in order to learn effectively. Coupled with experience must be plenty of opportunity to enrich their language, both as to the full meaning of words themselves and to the use of language as a way of communicating with others. Most children at this age can, to some extent, see another's point of view but only in a simple fashion. Thus, by the age of six, most children are ready to move into and become involved in the world of school, especially if it is one in which the teacher provides a rich variety of activities and experiences for them, with an emphasis on doing rather than on listening, and also remembers that, despite their competence and apparent independence, they still need to feel secure and important in their own right.

Children of this age group in developing societies
The wide range of individual differences within an age group of children has been stressed throughout this book. Teachers in Third World and plural countries need to be especially aware of home and environmental factors which may have a particular effect on children about to start their formal schooling. This means that they must make themselves very knowledgeable about the home background, experiences and expectations of their new pupils. All that we can do here is to focus attention on just a few of the more important and common aspects to be considered when planning the early school careers of your pupils.

On the physical level, the teacher will need to consider several features. For example, in many newly independent countries, where compulsory registration of births is not yet complete, there may be some doubt about the children's actual ages, especially in rural areas. Teachers will need to ensure that they do not assume that the children who appear either very advanced or immature for their recorded age, are in fact either advanced or retarded. The recorded age may differ from the real one by several months and the teacher must build his expectations from each child in the light of this possibility, assessing the actual competence that they show. Nutrition is another point to consider, both in relation to the local food customs and to the nutrition of individual children. In Third World countries even very young children often have to walk long distances to school. Not only is this in itself very tiring but in some circumstances they have not had much food to eat before starting out because the family custom is to have the first meal of the day at mid-morning. There is a close link between a child's (and indeed an adult's) ability to concentrate and how physically tired and hungry he is. A teacher must find out what the likely circumstances are for the children he teaches, especially at the younger ages. The actual solution to the problems of fatigue and nutrition can only be made in the specific circumstances, but consideration could be given to such measures as persuading parents to give children an adequate meal before they leave home, or to provide a nourishing but inexpensive protein supplement drink (there are several on the market). The teacher could make sure that there are adequate breaks during the school day for food and plan the timetable so that even the adequately fed child, who has had a long and early walk to get to school, has a chance to build up his energy before being given demanding learning tasks to do.

Teachers should also become aware of the possibility of more serious and longer-term malnutrition, which may be confined to a few individuals or be more wide-spread. In the poorer and less developed areas of some countries many children have not been fed enough of the right sort of protein during their early post-weaning years. It is thought that severe protein deficiency can impair the full development of mental powers, possibly permanently. A child's pre-school experiences, in his home and local community, can also affect his muscular capacities on entering school. He may be less able than others to hold and control a pencil and less skilful in other fine muscular movements. There are still many homes in which children have only little pre-school experience of such things. Those who have been fortunate enough to go to a nursery school have a distinct advantage. The others will need consideration and help to ensure that they do not become discouraged because of their lack of skill. Even wearing unaccustomed school clothing could present a problem to the new school child.

On the more recognizably intellectual level, pre-school experience within the home and community are important. This applies firstly to the sorts of knowledge which the child has acquired from his environment and obviously will vary according to his home's geographical location. Urban children may know little about rural matters and *vice versa*. Children from areas where there is little twentieth century technology will differ from those from more sophisticated areas. Secondly, and probably more significantly, home experience greatly influences a child's language development, its complexity and the ease with which he can use it to communicate ideas and as a vehicle of thought. He may have learned a particular variant or dialect of the language which the school uses, which, unless the teacher is aware of this and makes the necessary allowances for it, may cause problems. He may even have a home language entirely different from the language of the school or the wider country. The problems of learning and teaching in a second language will be dealt with in more detail later on, though it is worth your while considering at this stage whether it is preferable for young children to be taught through the medium of their home language at first, learning later through the official language, if these differ. Tied up with the use of language as well as with attitudes towards, and expectations from, schooling, is the readiness with which children will ask questions, either out of curiosity and the need to know, or for clarification when they do not understand. There are considerable family and cultural differences in the willingness of adults to listen to children talking, and to answer their questions. Indeed there are subcultures in which it is considered beneath the dignity of an adult, even a parent, to answer children's questions in a serious way. Such an attitude could well be carried into the school, stifling the natural curiosity which is the major motivator for learning, as well as encouraging conformity and the passive acceptance of the teacher's utterances, which we have seen is counter-productive to sound learning and to the development of intellectual competence in general.

Individual variation in physical development and competence are more easily managed by teachers than some other aspects of pre-school opportunity which are more likely to be encountered in developing than in developed countries. For example, all children come to school with expectations formed by their parents, older siblings and friends. Often such expectations are developed by adults who themselves experienced either no schooling or one very different from the present one. Unfortunately schools in developing countries, in the past, were often poorly equipped and overcrowded, the teachers doing their best despite a limited training for the job. To survive, they often had to insist on children sitting still in large classes and learning largely by rote; independent action, indeed activity itself, had to be strictly limited and punishment for non-conformity relatively severe. But, as we have seen, effective education involves action and independence, scope for imagination and curiosity and so on. Teachers in Third World countries may have a particular problem to overcome in changing their pupils' initial behaviour in school, which could derive from outdated expectations, reinforced by child-rearing practices which emphasize conformity and a respect verging on awe for someone with the authority of the teacher.

Of course, not all developing countries, or every area in the same country, conform to the picture painted above. In some cultures and sub-cultures, childhood is so valued that children are given very little formal discipline and are allowed to behave much as they like. This situation presents its own problems, which can be overcome by the sensitive teacher who has made himself aware of the cultural norms. Teachers in urban settings are likely to encounter children with a wider range of expectations, attitudes and behaviours than those in rural areas, variation which is often made more difficult to manage by a wider range of socio-economic levels in their homes, and of pre-school facilities such as nursery schools, play groups, etc.. Even the tendency of traditional extended families to exist in rural areas and nuclear families in urban areas can affect a child on his first arrival at school.

The child's experience of a literate culture, as gained from his home, influences his readiness to learn to read and write, a consideration by no means confined to developing countries though one likely to be exaggerated in them. Children who have seen adults and older children read and write with enjoyment, and who have themselves been read to and had first hand experience with books, are at a considerable advantage. There is even some evidence to suggest that a person's later ability to make sense of two dimensional pictures, both drawings and photographs, depends to some extent on opportunities that he has had, in his early years, to look at and talk about pictures. A teacher must never take such a skill for granted when his pupils come from homes with a limited level of literacy and access to written and illustrated material.

A final point of some significance, even at the start of a child's school career, is the possibility of sex differences in expectation and competence, many of which are encouraged by his home and cultural environment. The teacher will need to decide what these are, how far they ought to be counteracted by the school experience and how far they may be necessary to enable the child to adjust to his real world. A good general principle is that, if a particular expectation of sex differences in abilities and skills does now, or will in future, handicap the development of the full potential of either boys or girls, it should be firmly discouraged right from the start. For example, a phenomenon likely to be manifest later which is often, though not only, found in developing countries, is what has been termed 'learned incompetence' by girls when compared with boys, or by whole sub-groups, both male and female, when compared with other groups in the community. Every teacher must not only study the local situation but also examine his own attitudes towards and expectations of such groups to make sure that he does not unconsciously believe the myth of the in-born incompetence of certain defined groups.

The foregoing is by no means an exhaustive account of the areas in which teachers may need to make special provision for their young pupils, but I hope that it is sufficiently detailed to convince you that, as a teacher, your initial and most important consideration is the children whom you are to teach. Only when you have some real knowledge of them will you be able to decide what they need to learn and how best to help them to learn it.

The child from six to twelve years

It must be emphasized again that the ages selected are very general. There is no sudden change at the end of one period; instead there is a very gradual merger and even teachers often realize the extent of the change that has taken place in their pupils only when they compare the maturity of those who have been in their class for a year with the maturity of a new group coming in who are the same age as the outgoing group was a year earlier. The average age of six years is chosen because it is about the time in most countries when children first enter school and because it is about the age when important, new, intellectual and other possibilities seem to mature which make them able to take advantage of the new experiences of school, which in turn helps the further maturing of abilities.

This period is usually one in which physical growth continues steadily without any of the sudden spurts which characterize later childhood. It is a time when the physical skills of boys and girls are being developed. Both sexes learn a high level of control of their muscles and their co-ordination with each other and with their eyes. Boys and girls may begin to differ in the skills that they develop as a result of the different activities that their homes and cultures expect of them. For example rural boys are likely to have much more opportunity to run, jump, throw things, than do their sisters, who may well have domestic duties which develop other skills. Quite small girls are seen balancing pots on their heads with great poise and control, or carefully preparing food, weaving or crocheting. In contrast they may be relatively clumsy when running or climbing, whereas boys may find difficulty with activities needing fine finger control. Urban children may well have different areas of skill and clumsiness from rural ones. Only someone who knows the particular requirements of a community can identify the details. Occasionally, problems of eyesight may show up during this period, especially short-sightedness which is the result of the distance between the front and the back of the eye being a little too long to allow clear focussing. Such problems are easily corrected with glasses but may need an observant teacher to detect at first.

Towards the end of this period some children begin to show symptoms of adolescence; this is more likely in girls than in boys and usually starts with a fairly sudden spurt in physical growth. There is considerable and quite normal variation in the time of the visible onset of puberty though bodily changes have been quietly taking place for quite a while. The major significance for the teacher at this time is that the rapid increase in size and the substantial changes taking place internally, especially in the reproductive system of both boys and girls, can consume large amounts of energy which may for a time leave less available for concentration on school work. Teachers must be sensitive to this possibility; on the other hand, flagging energies can usually be revived by interesting and absorbing activity and it is not always of benefit to be too ready to blame lowered performance on the troubles of early adolescence.

Socially, this also seems to be a time of quiet improvement. Once the shock of starting school has worn off, most children gradually and happily expand their range of social contacts, becoming more involved with others of the same age, though still remaining very much a part of, and involved with, their own families, both extended and nuclear. This is a time of experimenting with friendships, learning more about how others react to them and thus continually modifying their behaviour and attitudes in response to the reaction of others of their own age group and of other adults. Everyone needs to learn about himself, his own strengths and weaknesses, so that he can build up a realistic 'mental model' of himself, often called the 'self concept', as a standard against which to assess his own behaviour. We can learn about ourselves only from the way others react to us and important developments begin to take place during these years in response to the 'messages' about ourselves which we receive from members of our own families, fellow pupils and teachers. Everyone has psychological needs which must be fulfilled satisfactorily if he is to grow into a mature, balanced person. These needs include not only a secure place within a loving family but also recognition by others of his personal worth within a realistic picture of himself. While the greatest contribution to the self concept is probably made during adolescence, the foundations are laid during the pre-adolescent period and the teacher has the task of giving each child the opportunity to develop self confidence and to feel that even though he may not be the most academically able person in the class, he has achieved many important things and in any case is a person worthy of other people's attention and effort on his behalf. He needs to feel important (though not more so than others) and allowed to accept increasing responsibility within his personal limitations.

During this period there is usually a voluntary separation of the sexes, boys playing with boys and girls with girls, though the separation is by no means complete in most cultures. Children are by now aware of their gender (sex); boys are usually glad that they are boys especially in male-dominated societies. Girls, on the other hand are usually accepting of their lot, taking their roles and responsibilities for granted even when they seem to be less exciting than those of their brothers.

Intellectually, important developments take place throughout this period. The child becomes progressively more able to deal with more complex ideas and to see the relationships between different asects of the same event, more detail of which will be given when discussing intellectual development. They make great strides in developing their knowledge of words and their meaning, as well as their general language use. By the end of the period they have developed the capacity to talk in complex and grammatically sound ways and the meaning of much of their vocabulary has become refined and enriched so that they can communicate with considerable accuracy. In fact, they have acquired virtually all the intellectual skills of an adult, which does not mean that they can be expected to learn anything which an adult can learn and in the same way, because they have not yet fully developed the capacity to deal with abstract, non-concrete ideas. They still need almost all their learning to be strongly practical, based, as far as possible, on direct experience rather than on verbal descriptions of things and events beyond their experience. There is some argument as to whether their need for so much direct experience is merely because their knowledge of the world is still very far from complete or because the capacity to deal with abstract ideas has not yet matured physically. Whichever is the truth of the matter you will be a more successful teacher and your pupils will be more successful learners if you make their learning as real and direct as possible, while, especially towards the end of this period, asking them questions and pointing out some theoretical possibilities which will lead them towards being able to use higher levels of reasoning at a later stage.

Children in this age group in Third World and plural countries
Many of the topics which are of particular concern to teachers in Third World countries apply to all ages so that you are advised to look back at the earlier age group to help you to decide whether any of the suggestions given apply to the children in your care. Aspects of topics of particular relevance to adolescence will be discussed in the next section, but some of them may be of importance to the age group under discussion here.

Nutrition and fatigue, because of the distance some children have to walk to school, must still be considered where appropriate, especially among the younger ones of this age group. Many children, perhaps rural more than urban, may also be tired because of the domestic responsibilities that they have, such as looking after livestock, taking care of younger brothers and sisters, etc.. As was suggested earlier, the solution to such problems is not necessarily to expect less of such children, because of the long-term handicap that this could bring, but as far as is possible to arrange the timetable and the day's activities so that the more demanding work is given when energies are highest. Opportunities for eating need to be sensibly arranged. In some countries teachers have successfully persuaded parents to modify the eating and rest patterns of their children so as to give them every chance to make the most of their educational opportunities.

During this period when children, especially boys, are allowed more freedom in their home areas, there is a greater possibility of them acquiring parasitic diseases such as Bilharzia (schistosomiasis), which is endemic in the open waters of Africa and parts of South America, and hookworm. In some countries, diseases such as malaria can be widespread despite efforts to control them environmentally and through medication. All such diseases can seriously reduce a child's ability to concentrate on school work and are more of a problem because in their mild form they are not easily detected by signs other than general tiredness and lack of interest in things which require mental and physical effort. Their effects are not only the immediate ones of poor classroom performance; they also have a less direct effect in that they can prevent children from being interested in and reactive to their wider environment, thus depriving them of the chance to enrich their knowledge and develop their intellectual potential further.

The teacher's responsibility here is wider than merely trying to help the child in the classroom and must include encouraging parents to seek medical help when their children appear to be always tired. The school programme must include health education to enable children to reduce the possibility of infection. In the classroom the teacher should not add to the child's unhappiness by being unduly harsh with him if he is unable to concentrate because of a weakening disease but he should arrange the day's programme to take advantage of times when energy is highest. The author undertook research into the classroom effects of heavy Bilharzia infection and discovered that the main symptoms of fatigue could to some extent be overcome if the children were highly motivated and interested. The routine and rather dull lessons which even healthy children found uninspiring but in which they could be pushed into reasonable activity, were just too much of an effort for the Bilharzia sufferers.

Social considerations at this stage are much the same as at the previous one, although the effects of certain customs are likely to be increased. Parental and pupil expectations of the school can be an increasing problem, especially since schooling is still widely seen by many parents, and some teachers, as exclusively the process whereby children can be taught enough to pass examinations and obtain certificates which will give them a better chance in the competitive adult world. Children soon gather the idea that anything in the curriculum which is not directed towards such a goal is a waste of time, an attitude which can have a significant influence on their motivation to learn. This can take two main forms, firstly, lowered effort in apparently non-essentials and secondly, an excessive willingness to accept, or even demand, teaching methods which they think will cram them full of the information and skills which they need to pass the examinations. Often the children interpret the more interesting teaching methods which involve them in enjoyable exploratory activity as a waste of time, an opinion often reinforced by parents. Teachers themselves may find it difficult to overcome such attitudes, perhaps because their own manifestly successful educational experiences were often similar. Teachers need to be very aware of this possibility and to develop confidence in the long-term effectiveness of more pupil-involved learning methods and a curriculum which aims at aiding many aspects of a child's development and not merely the narrow academic one of acquiring factual knowledge.

The extent to which adults, and especially teachers, are regarded as special people whose authority must not be questioned could have an increasing effect during this period. In some cases, where such conformity is encouraged, children could be handicapped in their school progress because it reduces the need to think, to question, to observe and to experiment with some independence. This, in turn, reduces the effectiveness with which intellectual capacities are developed and used. Here again is a temptation for the teacher, especially one who is confronted with a large class and full timetable, to take advantage of the conformity and quiet acceptance of unadventurous teaching, a possibility of which he must become aware. His life is made more difficult if he has in his class some children who are traditionally conformist and others from more stimulating and forward-thinking homes who become restless if not allowed to become positively involved in active learning. Quite often, in communities where girls are expected to be quiet and non-competitive in the presence of boys, the teacher will have to take steps to ensure that the former are not handicapped, either by their non-involvement in class activities or by his own concept of their role and intellectual capacities. There is some evidence that in communities where a girl's traditional role is a very passive one, single sex rather than co-educational schooling is preferable, especially if their teachers are committed to the idea that girls are as educable as boys and need and deserve similar opportunities.

Inevitably the social influences on a child's development have intellectual effects, some of which have been at least implied in the foregoing paragraph. The extent to which parents and other adults in the community interact with children and the sort of verbal experiences that they share are important, both because of the interest in, and knowledge of, the outside world created and the language knowledge and usage developed. At this stage, both through traditional stories and adult conversation, children learn quite a lot about how the world around them works, the causation of many natural phenomena, etc. as well as about whatever technology is available in the community. All human groups, in developed as well as in developing countries, have an extensive collection of myths and folk-lore. There is less chance in developing countries, especially in the remoter rural areas, for children to separate in their minds what is myth and fiction and what is scientific fact. This can pose problems when, towards the end of this stage and later, in adolescence, they need to look at the world more scientifically. The myth may give an explanation different from the one which knowledge gives, leading to confusion in the minds of children especially when a number of adults in their families hold the myths to be literally true. For example, there are many groups which traditionally accept that evil spirits can cause disease or crop disaster, whereas modern science has shown that the real cause is dietary or soil deficiency, or the presence of harmful micro-organisms. A strong traditional belief cannot be dismissed just by the teacher's word. He will need to know what the traditional beliefs are and help the pupils to put them into perspective. Again, it is knowledge of the local community which the teacher needs as a starting point to his teaching.

There is evidence to suggest that certain environments and the intellectual demands that they make on the developing child can affect the efficiency of certain intellectual capacities and ways of functioning. These include, for example, the ability to understand and think about shapes, spaces and numbers. Research suggests that children from groups whose child rearing practices tend to restrict their physical exploration of their immediate environment from the earliest months of their lives, may not develop their full potential for spatial reasoning, an essential ingredient in mathematical, technical and scientific competence. Abilities to think and act creatively and imaginatively may also reflect cultural expectations and opportunities. A deeper consideration of these and related aspects of intellectual development and function will be discussed in more detail when dealing with cognitive development. The effects of such influences, some of which are stronger in Third World than in older, industrialised countries, often begin to show themselves at this stage, but preventative and curative measures can also be effective if adopted by teachers early enough.

The adolescent and young person

In contrast to the relatively steady and undramatic changes which took place during the previous few years, the changes which occur during the next few are little short of spectacular. We must remind ourselves again of the wide range of completely normal individual differences in the age and rate at which development takes place, concentrating instead on the order and meaning of its symptoms. The most obvious and important development is that of sexual maturity and the changes in bodily size, proportion and function which go with it. On average, girls enter and complete puberty earlier than boys. The balance of their body changes, the breasts and thighs becoming relatively heavier and less manageable, leading to some embarrassing clumsiness until they become used to their new shape and able to control it. Until the additional hormones (chemicals, produced by the body, which are responsible for the many changes) have achieved a balance, a girl may feel out of proportion, with too much weight on some parts of the body and greasy, unattractive skin and hair. Full height is usually attained and the process of becoming sexually mature completed by the mid-teens, though some changes in the final body shape may continue for a while. The rapid rate at which the physical changes take place may lead to unusual tiredness and there may be a weakening irregularity in menstruation and teachers need to understand this. Contrary to popular belief, however, there is rarely need to make special allowances for this in normal school activities. Indeed, it has been shown that too much obvious allowance being made for adolescence in girls can make them believe that they have cause for concern and lead them to expect and look for problems and thus lower their achievement. A matter of fact approach,

5 *Teenagers practising football skills*

combined with unobtrusive observation for exceptional cases, which may need some medical advice, is the most effective attitude to adopt.

Boys, too, experience a rapid change in the balance and proportions of their bodies, the most noticeable being the relative lengths of their legs and arms, which grow exceptionally fast and which, as with girls, take some getting used to. Boys, too, may have times when they seem to be lacking in energy but, if this is too frequent, the cause may lie elsewhere and warrant medical examination. Puberty in boys and increase in physical growth often goes on into the late teens, though sexual maturity is usually attained before the full height is reached.

The age at which puberty becomes manifest varies from culture to culture and social class to social class. The healthier the living circumstances, especially as regards nutrition, rest and absence of disease, the earlier is the average age of puberty likely to be, though early or late puberty in an individual case is not necessarily related to nutrition, health etc.. It is most likely that the earliest time at which puberty can occur is determined by one's family inheritance. As was mentioned in an earlier chapter, children in Western industrialised countries now become physically mature several years earlier than they did at the end of the nineteenth century and the gap between the more and less wealthy is almost non-existent. The same appears to be happening in newer countries, especially among people whose nutrition and health facilities are good. The average height of the adult population in richer countries has increased by several inches over the same period.

The adolescent has to make social and emotional adjustments to the physical changes which are taking place. For example, the temporary clumsiness which may be experienced until final bodily proportions are reached may be briefly embarrassing to some. The individual who enters puberty at an earlier age than most of his or her contemporaries may experience particular problems both in adapting his activities so that he can fit in with his smaller friends and in being conspicuous in a group. Adults may increase the problems by expecting him or her to behave like someone older than the actual age. In most societies, a boy who matures early, physically, is less likely to feel handicapped than a girl, because size and strength are valued male characteristics. On the other hand, a late-maturing boy could suffer stress because he seems to remain a child longer than his friends. Late-maturing girls seem to be less concerned but they too need assurance that their delayed development is perfectly normal. Obviously any form of stress and concern about oneself can divert attention and energy from school learning so that teachers of adolescents should help them to understand the implications of the bodily changes and the normality of individual differences.

During this period the adolescent develops a strong sense of self-awareness and is very concerned about the sort of person he is and how other people see him. He has built up, over the years, from clues given him by his family, friends, neighbours, school, books and mass media, a mental picture of what type of person he should ideally be. He has also been building up, from the same clues, a picture of what he himself is, his strengths and weaknesses, his level of acceptability to others and how he is likely to behave in various circumstances. Such a self concept will include, not merely specific actions that he will take, but attitudes and motives, especially those which influence his school behaviour and learning. His ideal self and actual self are constantly changing as his experiences widen, and stress and unhappiness, or even behaviour problems, can occur if the difference between them is too great. It must be emphasized that, although almost all adolescents go through periods when they are distressed about their acceptability to themselves and others, most manage to handle this difficult time adequately, especially when they have a stable, secure home and an understanding school environment which recognizes and caters for their developing needs.

Despite the fact that the adolescent still needs a satisfactory home in his background, he spends an increasing amount of time in the company of his friends and school fellows and attaches increasing weight to their activities and social and moral values, which sometimes conflict with those of the home and school. Young people need this involvement with such groups, partly because it gives them a sense of belonging to a group which accepts them. Groups offer an opportunity of learning more about social inter-relationships and how to adapt to others and, because there is no generation gap between members of the group as there is between them and adults, they feel less threatened and frustrated. Adolescents often belong to more than one peer group, one of them being of the same sex as themselves and the other being of mixed sex, the latter growing in importance as time passes.

During these years, not only is the general self concept developed and refined but so is the sex role expected of them, which of course varies from one socio-economic and ethnic group to another. But the adolescent who is not a member of a peer group is often an unhappy and even deprived person.

During adolescence, additional and important intellectual functions may develop and mature. As was mentioned earlier, pre-adolescent children usually have only a limited competence in learning through abstract ideas, especially those of which they have had little first hand experience. There is evidence to suggest that during adolescence the ability to think about and reason with ideas may develop so that the individual will be increasingly able to understand complicated ideas and to make sensible judgements and decisions about how to act based on careful analysis of all the relevant circumstances. It is obvious that this is a very necessary adult, intellectual and social skill and is thus very important for education and the teacher. The technical term for this aspect of mental function is Formal Operational Reasoning because of its concern with the form of the thinking processes as well as with the form in which the mental ingredients are operated on. This is a difficult concept which it is hoped will become clearer in a later chapter.

You will have noticed in the previous paragraph that I emphasized the word *may* rather than *will* when talking about the development of thinking and reasoning skills. For a number of reasons, not all, or even most, adults develop their formal thinking skills to the full, continuing to reason effectively much of the time in practical and direct terms. At present, the important thing for the teacher of adolescents to remember is that formal reasoning competence does not develop far by itself but requires opportunities for learning how to use and practise it. This implies that all adolescents, and especially younger ones, still need much of their learning to take place in real and practical situations in which ideas are made as directly and personally meaningful to them as possible. Once they have a basis of direct experience, they can be encouraged by their teachers to identify basic principles and try them out in new situations, or relate them to other principles to enable them to reach general conclusions about cause and effect. A great deal of secondary teaching is still too remote for many pupils, the teacher often being concerned with ensuring that their learners remember a collection of pre-determined facts, an educational objective which all too often not only does not encourage intellectual development but positively handicaps it.

This is a period, too, during which particular mental abilities and disabilities may become more evident, though it is not clear whether this is essentially in-born and hence inevitable, or whether diverging individual motives, interests and expectations, together with a greater independence of choice, is the major cause. This divergence of abilities includes areas of learning such as the scientific, technical and mathematical fields, or the verbal, artistic and practical ones. It also includes ways in which individuals approach learning tasks and problems. For example, some habitually look at a problem or situation as a whole, whereas others habitually analyse its components and may not see the whole too clearly. The willingness to be imaginatively and creatively original increases in some and decreases in others until fairly stable individual patterns are established.

Thus, adolescence is a very important period, physically, socially and intellectually, the school as well as the home having a very important part to play in helping young people to become mature, balanced and thinking adults. Although all stages of development are important in themselves and have a strong bearing on later possibilities, the adolescent stage and the social and educational opportunities which are available bring together all facets and integrate them into a whole human being. During the later adolescent years, the individual moves into adulthood, which is not so much a stage of personal maturity but a status conferred by society. Nevertheless, once formal schooling stops the maturing process continues, moulded by the demands made by personal circumstances; the way in which the maturing continues is determined by the direction set earlier.

Young people in this age group in plural and Third World countries

Adolescence and many of its social and emotional symptoms have been widely studied to determine the extent that different social, cultural and ethnic circumstances may be influential on behaviour and adjustment. Social anthropologists, such as Margaret Mead and Ruth Benedict working several decades ago, concluded that many of the problems of young people in industrialised countries did not exist in rural societies which had experienced relatively little change in their way of life, customs and family structure. It was argued that adolescents in such societies, many of which had traditional 'coming of age' ceremonies which marked an abrupt and complete change from childhood to adulthood, had a more clearly defined and comprehensible role in their families and neighbourhoods. They were thus less likely to show signs of rebellion and discontent than adolescents were reported to show in industrialised and rapidly changing societies. Although recent work designed to test the observations and hypotheses of such anthropologists have by no means supported the original work or the conclusions, there are nevertheless many indications that adolescents are particularly affected by the confusion and discrepancies which can arise when their status as people is not clearly defined and when they are required to adapt their behaviour and expectations to a wide range of different circumstances. In the so-called developed countries an adolescent's life contains much to which he has to adapt; at times he is still seen as a child, dependent on parents and under the authority of the school, while at others he is seen as near adult and hence expected to behave responsibly. He wants to be considered part of the adult world but still needs to acquire many adult skills. It is little wonder, then, that some (in fact surprisingly few) find real difficulty in coming to terms with their lives and so cause problems for themselves and adults.

In Third World countries the same mechanisms are often at work, but in exaggerated form because the rate of change, for urban young people even more than those who remain in rural areas, is often very rapid indeed and the gap between the lives lived by parents and their adolescent children is often greater than that in more industrialised and technologically-developed countries. The generation gap widens still further when the impact of the outside world, as well as of an increasingly sophisticated education system, encourages the young to question many of the religious and philosophical beliefs of their parents and extended family. An understandable result is that some adolescents seem arrogant towards their elders and their less sophisticated relatives, causing friction and unhappiness. One of the effects of becoming literate and experiencing several years of schooling, especially of the sort which encourages one to think, question and explore, is the development of thinking skills and logical processes which less fortunate adults may not be able to use to such telling effect. The possible detrimental effects touch both adult and adolescent, the former perhaps losing some confidence in his relationships with his children and the latter building up an exaggeratedly optimistic self-image. Thus the possible social effects of rapid development and educational opportunity need special consideration by teachers of adolescents who, while not doing anything to slow down progress, should help their pupils to understand the processes of change and to retain their respect for their parents and others.

Another problem more likely to be met in developing than in developed countries is that of centralized secondary schools enrolling children from a variety of primary schools, from the remotely rural to the completely urban. The homes from which the pupils come is just as wide-ranging and to cater for children from such a diversity of backgrounds is a particularly difficult task, since effective learning begins from the learner's existing knowledge and experience. While nowhere in the world is there a group of learners of identical knowledge and experience, children in long-established communities normally have a reasonably similar base on which to establish new learning. Teachers, too, are most frequently fairly knowledgeable about the children's background and in touch with it themselves. This may not be the case in Third World countries and plural communities, the difficulty being made worse when the school class contains culture groups and sub-groups with different home languages. It is likely that the teacher's own background experience is different again from many, if not most, of his pupils. There is no simple formula which can be given here to ensure that he succeeds in his task of teaching such a diverse group of pupils. All that can be done is to alert him to the difficulties and to urge him as before to become as knowledgeable as possible about his pupils, not making assumptions about their previous knowledge and experience without satisfying himself that they are justified.

Differences between individuals tend to widen as they get older so that cultural and environmental factors which encourage or restrict the development of special skills and abilities can have an exaggerated effect during adolescence. This may apply, for example, to the school attitudes and expectations of girls compared with boys, especially in cultures where these are significantly different from each other. A further problem more frequently found in non-technological than in technological societies and which is particularly significant at adolescence, is in the ease with which pupils can think about and understand shapes and spaces, and interpret two dimensional plans, diagrams, graphs and maps. Spatial reasoning is a necessary skill for a high level of achievement in scientific, mathematical and technical subjects. Teachers should not assume that their pupils are all able to understand diagrams, maps, etc. without further tuition. Equally, adolescents from traditional rural communities in less-developed countries often have an exceptionally well-developed verbal facility, able to remember what has been heard or read very efficiently and to discuss complex questions articulately. Boys often show this facility more than girls, especially when they live in male-dominated societies. While such abilities are valuable and should be encouraged to develop, there is a temptation for secondary school teachers to take advantage of the pupils' willingness to listen and their ability to absorb information from lecture-type lessons. Over-use of such teaching techniques may limit the learner's opportunities to develop his formal reasoning skills and his spatial and technical competences, substituting a diet of factual knowledge for true intellectual development and skill in adult reasoning, decision making and judgement forming.

Application 11

Arrange to spend several hours in a school, or in classes catering for each of the following groups:
   pre-school ... approximate ages 3 to 6 years
   lower primary or infants ... approximate ages 6 to 8 years
   upper primary ... approximate ages 8 to 12 years
   secondary ... approximate ages 12 to 16 years.

Watch the children working in their groups or classes, and mix with them quietly during their less formal work and play times. Make a particular point of comparing the behaviour of the youngest children in each age range with that of the oldest in that range. Compare, too, the oldest of one age group with the youngest of the next group.

Make notes of your observations, *for boys and girls separately* and include them in your personal file, using the following guidelines:

1 In class lessons

How long on the average do they pay attention to one activity?
What seems to hold their attention the longest and what do they seem to find it hard to concentrate on?
Which classroom activities or learning methods do they seem to find easiest and which most difficult, whether or not they can concentrate on them?
How willing are they, on average, to contribute to the lesson with speech, by volunteering to answer or ask questions, to make comments or to offer other information?
How well do they control their pen or pencil?
Ask them to draw a man or woman on a piece of paper which you should give them, but do not give any instructions on how to do it. Collect the drawings and compare them with those produced by children of other ages, not only for the quality of the drawing but also for the accuracy and complexity of the picture itself.

What do the children think is good and bad behaviour? Is it the same as the teacher's idea, or your own idea, of good and bad behaviour? What is their attitude to the teacher... friendly, open and trusting or rather nervous and fearful, or merely neutral?

2 Out of class

What do most of the children do during their free play time, what games do they play, what sort of children make up the groups and how often do the members of groups change?

How physically competent, co-ordinated and confident are the children?

What is their apparent attitude to toys and other available materials? Do they share them freely, try to keep them to themselves, fight with others about them, etc.?

How much and in what way do they talk to each other, either in pairs or in bigger groups? What things do they talk about and how much do they listen to or argue with each other?

What are their reactions to you, a stranger? Are they friendly, shy, fearful, indifferent etc.?

Add to the observations proposed above any others that you find interesting and important. When making your comments add some further information to indicate the basis for your conclusions about an activity. As your experience grows it would be useful for you to look again and revise or enlarge on your earlier observations.

If at all possible, compare notes with fellow students who observed different children, to see how general your findings are. Propose possible causes of any major variation that you may find.

Further reading

Now that you have read a general account of child development and looked at some children in their school settings at selected points in their progress towards adulthood, you should read more deeply about the age group which you are most likely to teach. Below are some suggested references from general texts, though you may find others in your own library. Unfortunately, most do not discuss aspects of special importance to your own country. You should get in touch with, for example, the Education Department at a university or major college in your own area and ask for information about books and journals which record local research or describe local development patterns. Some major international universities may have research centres with information relevant to your own needs.

There are several interesting and useful papers in Wagner and Stevenson (see page 37 for full reference) which would be worth reading, especially Super, C.M. and Harkness, S., 'The Development of Affect in

Infancy and Early Childhood', (p 1) and Blount, B.G., 'Culture and the Language of Socialization: parental speech.', (p 54).

Look in your library for a general text on child development and read particularly about the age groups whom you expect to teach. Remember, however, that such texts deal with averages and often concentrate on children from Western countries. As long as you read such texts while applying what is written to the children in your country, you will increase your awareness of child development and its general patterns. One such text is Hurlock, Elizabeth, *Child Development*, (Fourth Edition), New York, McGraw-Hill Book Company, 1964.

CHAPTER SIX

Helping learning to take place

Motivating pupils to learn

You should now be ready to look more closely at how best to ensure that your pupils learn what is required of them. The first point to consider is how to make them settle down to the task and to pay attention to it in such a way that they succeed in achieving the learning objectives that you have set for them. The term for this process is *motivation*, a word meaning something like 'move into action'. Unless a teacher can 'move his pupils to act' in the way that he wants them to he will not be very successful in his job. Of course, motivation is not confined only to the classroom but comes into all our activities and is a very complex subject, mainly because we are all motivated by different things, even when undertaking the same task. Moreover, it is very difficult to analyse our own motives for anything that we do; analysing other people's motives so that we can make use of them is even more difficult.

Extrinsic motivation

Think for a moment of your own motives for studying educational psychology. Because you are a mature adult you are able to see further ahead than most school children and can accept more abstract and long term motives than they can. You probably accept that in order to succeed in your teacher training course you need to know and understand the information and ideas included in it, whether or not it is entertaining and interesting or deals with important questions to which you feel the need to know the answers. You are able to put off doing things which you find more pleasurable, such as talking with your friends, playing football or reading a novel, because you recognize that if you want to achieve a longer term goal, such as becoming a qualified teacher and thus obtaining a reasonably well paid job, you will have to put effort into the requirements of your course. There may be other motives, too. For example, you want to be successful in your course and so retain your self-respect and the respect of others whom you care about. The amount of effort which you put into your study will, to some extent, be determined by whether you are content to stay with the crowd or whether you want to be seen, by yourself and others, as among the highest achievers in your group. You may also include among your own motives, not merely the eventual goals of a good job and a sense of achievement (and its opposite, the fear of failure), but a real curiosity about how people come to behave as they do and a desire to improve their lives through your teaching.

The important point that arises from the foregoing discussion, and probably most other motives that you can identify in yourself, is that they are largely in your own hands and are to some extent outside the content of the educational psychology course itself and the learning activities that you have to complete in order to be successful. This sort of motivation is called *extrinsic*, the learning being mainly a means to a clear objective; the motivation to learn does not directly come from the material to be learned. On the other hand, even the most strongly extrinsically motivated student can be more successful in his learning if the material is presented, and the learning activities planned, so that they give satisfaction and pleasure in themselves and can be seen by the student as important to him.

In contrast to the adult learner, the child in school often has very little choice about attendance, and what he has to learn. Only in adolescence can he begin to identify and perhaps accept longer term goals and so become voluntarily motivated. The teacher has the task of devising other ways of 'arousing the learners to action', the ways that he chooses being dependent on many things, such as the age and ability levels of the pupils, what naturally interests them and arouses their curiosity, how long they are able to concentrate on one activity, what things will extend their ability to concentrate, what skills and knowledge are important to them and what skills and knowledge they already have, what they expect school to be like and many other things. A teacher needs a great deal of background information about the developmental processes in children and about his particular pupils in order to motivate them to learn. *All lesson planning must start from this point rather than from the actual subject matter of the lesson.* The topic or skill to be learned is of course important but must be analysed in the light of knowledge of the learners rather than, as often happens, the other way round.

On a happier note, the teacher, especially of younger children, has the advantage in that, even though children may be in school because they have to be there, most of them accept, without question, that they are expected to do what the teacher asks of them, even though it may not be very exciting. Indeed, most children are more positive than this; they like and need an orderly life with someone to plan their use of time. This is not to suggest that even the youngest should be organized firmly in all their activities with no flexibility or personal choice. It means that, provided that what they are expected to do is within their abilities and expectations, most are willing to make a reasonable effort. Then, too, most of them really do want to learn at least some of the skills offered, particularly when they first start school. They *want* to be able to read and write and 'do sums' like their brothers, sisters and friends, and are willing to work at it. (Later we shall consider the special problems in learning which some children have, some of which are associated with motivation rather than disability). Then, too, most children, especially younger ones, have a strong sense of natural curiosity and wonder at the world around them, and this can be used by the knowledgeable teacher. As children grow older they are often more selective in the things which arouse their curiosity, making some teachers think that they have lost their curiosity and desire to learn. This is rarely the case; curiosity is still there but can be stifled in school by dull and unimaginative learning experiences. A teacher who has kept his own sense of excitement in learning is likely to be able to stimulate it in his pupils.

Intrinsic motivation

So far almost all that has been said about motivating pupils to learn has involved the extrinsic aspects. *Intrinsic* motivation is that which happens because either the matter to be learned is so interesting to the learner that he is carried along by it or the learning activities which have been planned are themselves exciting. The appeal is directly to something within the pupil himself. For example, reading an exciting story, listening to a lively account of an historical event or watching it on film, painting a picture or making a model can carry their own motivators. Intrinsic motivation is not always effortless and can be very demanding as, for example, when a pupil in a science class performs experiments to discover the answer to a question that interests him, or wrestles with a difficult mathematical problem. Often learning has to be extrinsically motivated by the teacher but then becomes intrinsically worthwhile, which in turn leads to further effort. The author's younger son, then aged about eight, was envious of his older brother's success in a story writing competition and wanted to win a prize for himself as well as the praise of his parents. After several false starts and almost giving up he suddenly found that the story took over and he spent all his spare time for several days in writing it, copying it neatly and drawing pictures to illustrate it, despite the fact that by that time he knew he was too late to enter the competition. Here is an example of the interaction between extrinsic and intrinsic motivation, from which it can be seen that the latter is the stronger, once it can be aroused, since it satisfies needs stemming from within the individual.

Positive and negative motivation

There is another way of looking at motivation, and that is whether it is *negative* or *positive*. *Negative motivation* is that which relies on some sort of real or suggested threat of something unpleasant happening if the learning is not achieved, or the necessary effort not made. This sort of motivation is not always bad, in that it often leads to reasonable achievement. Fear of failure in tests and examinations, or of the disapproval of teachers and parents may fall into this category. In countries where opportunities for post-primary or post-secondary education are limited and entry is competitive, such motivation is powerful for some pupils, but it can be destructive for others. While one can understand the basis of the motivation, there are dangers in over-using it to motivate one's pupils. It can limit their (and often the teacher's) efforts to subjects and topics likely to be examined, and lead to learning to answer questions rather than to developing wider curiosity and the capacity for exploration in their learning. Pupils who do not have much confidence in their own ability to succeed in such selection procedures may become either too anxious and so unable to concentrate fully, or they may tell themselves that they have no chance of passing so why make any effort to learn the examination material.

6 *An overcrowded classroom*

A less constructive use of negative motivation is made by the teacher who uses, or threatens to use, excessive punishment for failure to learn, whether it be physical punishment or some form of deprivation (i.e. not being allowed to have or do something which is enjoyed by the pupil). While one can understand the frustration of a teacher, especially one whose classes are large and whose facilities and time for preparation are limited, research shows that such negative motivation rarely gets to the root of the real learning problem because it assumes that the failure to learn is entirely the fault of the learner and can be corrected by more effort on his part. Punishment is assumed to produce the necessary effort, which it may sometimes do, though it is rarely a long term cure. Persistent failure to learn or to make an effort to do what is required should be analysed by the teacher in terms of the proven principles of successful learning, so that more suitable motivation methods can be used, and more appropriate learning tasks and objectives devised.

Positive motivation, on the other hand, does not rely on fear, excessive anxiety or the threat of being deprived of something enjoyable. It aims at making sure that the learner can expect

7 *A stimulating learning enviroment*

something pleasant to happen as a result of his efforts. This does not mean that there is always a direct reward or prize, if only because this suggests that where there are winners there are also losers, which is negative motivation for some. The best form of positive motivation is where the learner realizes that he will be able to achieve something worthwhile and recognizable, that his efforts will be appreciated and that the teacher thinks well enough of him to plan the learning especially and personally for him. Positive motivation is the result of the attitude of the teacher towards his pupils and is made clear to them in subtle ways which include, not only the preparation of learning activities which are likely to lead to success, but also the way that he knows and relates to each individual. The whole classroom setting and atmosphere is the main motivator here and research has shown that successful and respected teachers are the ones who build up a positive attitude towards learning, even by those children whose abilities are limited. They are people whose approval and respect the pupils wish to earn and keep, largely because they approve of and respect their pupils.

Pupils' expectations about their learning

Although the question of motivation has been dealt with on its own, it is important to remember that every aspect of a learning experience adds to, or subtracts from, the motivation of the learner to make the necessary effort. One of the major motivators for learning in school is the *expectation* by the learner that he will be successful, and all lessons should be planned so as to ensure, as far as possible, that everyone can see some progress in himself. This seems obvious. No teacher would deliberately plan and teach lessons which are not likely to be successfully learned by his pupils. On the other hand, there are several actions which a teacher can take which will increase the chances of successful learning. First of all, he should not expect all his pupils to find the learning equally easy and he should plan so that there is an opportunity for those needing more help, explanation or practice, to receive it, while others are occupied with further exploration of the topic on their own or in groups. He should plan very carefully how he intends to find out what has actually been learned and what needs more emphasis and for which pupils. If he has analysed the objectives of the lesson in practical terms (see page 7) the analysis of the resulting learning will be easier.

Secondly, it is important that the learners know what is expected of them, the purpose of the learning and what they should be able to do with it. It is not usually enough just to tell them what the lesson objectives are, in the way that you have written them in your lesson plan. There must be explanation, discussion and illustration until they are clear. Not only this, but the learners must also be able to see that the new knowledge or skill is an important part of the overall topic or the development of the final skill. Although clarifying the objectives may be only a small part of any single lesson, the teacher should always be sure that his pupils are really clear as to the why, what and how of their intended learning. The mere fact of focussing on these aspects of his preparation of lessons is likely to make the teacher select and organize the content of his lessons more logically and in a form likely to be suitable for his pupils. Preparation for teaching is usually more effective if the whole topic or skill is at first thought through even if it covers several timetabled periods. Only later should it be divided into separate lessons. The pupils can be given a brief survey of the whole topic and its objectives at the start of the series of lessons, with brief reminders in between to show how each part fits into the whole.

Learning and the pupil's needs

Successful learning also requires that, from the outset, the learner can see how it fits in with his own needs, existing knowledge and skills. Even completely new and unfamiliar ideas must somehow become attached to more familiar ones so as to reduce the insecurity that we all feel when we try to learn something entirely new, and teachers must consciously plan for this in their lessons. For example, when teaching a new process in arithmetic, such as subtraction, to young children, the idea can be introduced by starting the first lesson with some shopping games involving subtraction, until it can be seen that a quicker method is needed by shopkeepers. At this point very simple practical exercises are worked by both teacher and pupils together, followed by the pupils making up their own example. At a more advanced level, for example, introducing a new book into a literature course, the teacher might first find familiar and contemporary situations which involve events and motives similar to those appearing in the plot of the book, using these to arouse curiosity and to create some familiarity and relevance for the pupils.

New words which are essential to understand a scientific or technical principle should be put into familiar and practical situations. Dictionary definitions are usually too abstract and general to be of much real use to pupils. The word 'proportion', for example, is defined (in part) as 'relative magnitude', which is meaningless until learners have focussed on everyday situations in which the idea (or *concept*) of proportion can be easily seen. Often it stretches the teacher's imagination to find situations which are suitable jumping off points for new learning but, without them, learning is likely to be less successful, i.e. is remembered and applied to new situations. Learning which leads to early forgetting is usually that which depends heavily on pure memorising and is not taken in to become part of the pupil's store of knowledge and understanding.

The teacher's knowledge of the subject

A further, often overlooked, essential for arranging for successful learning is a high level of understanding of the subject matter by the teacher himself. It is important that he knows the structure of the subject, i.e. the ideas which build up logically to an understanding of it. It would be thought that teachers, because of their own history of successful study and training, will have the necessary knowledge, but research has shown that some quite basic ideas and principles have not been fully understood by some teachers and thus they may not be correctly analysed when the subject matter is being prepared for pupils to learn. For example, some teachers have not consciously realised that multiplication is really a short cut for addition when each item is the same. Many competent teachers are not clear why, when dividing vulgar fractions, one inverts the divisor and then uses the multiplication process. Others may not have fully realised, when teaching history, how the complex interaction of economic and geographical circumstances, social custom, historical rivalries and individual and group personality traits, often determined the direction that important events of the past took. Such teachers tend to concentrate on the sequence of events rather than their causes, thus missing opportunities of helping their pupils to understand their own world more clearly and to develop more analytic learning habits.

The result is that the learning experiences which they plan tend to become memory exercises rather than a logical series of consequences of interacting influences. Happily, research has also shown that, once the need to identify and understand the concepts and principles, which are essential if a topic is to be broken down into its parts to enable learning, is realised, most teachers can achieve it successfully, often to their own delighted surprise.

One often hears teachers, especially the successful ones, remark that they had never really understood a concept or process until they had to teach it to others. All this means that even at the lowest levels of the primary school, it is necessary for teachers to spend a considerable amount of time not only in selecting the next topic in the syllabus but also in analysing what concepts and knowledge must be conveyed if it is to be learned successfully. There is a logical pattern in most learning areas, later aspects depending on the successful understanding of earlier ones. Often this is obvious but teachers must be careful not to take its apparent obviousness for granted but must carefully break the topic down into its separate ideas in the order in which they must be learned. This task becomes increasingly complex as the emphasis moves from practical skills in the earlier years to the depth of content later on.

Learning how to learn

On several occasions in this book, the need for ensuring that the pupils learn how to learn is stressed. This is a long-term process as each learner gradually realises that some of the learning activities that he uses in the classroom are successful and satisfying while others are not. The method adopted for learning a particular skill or concept depends largely on what he expects to have to do to show that he has learned it. For example, if he knows that he will have to write a summary of the main events in a chapter in a history textbook he will look for those events and probably ignore motives and inter-relationships. If, on the other hand, he knows he will be expected, for example, to explain to the class what his point of view would be if he were actually present at an important incident in history, he is likely to approach the learning task from a human point of view, looking for arguments and opinions. Many lessons can be planned so that pupils can find some of the information for themselves and use it to solve problems and to answer questions, as alternatives to having the information supplied directly to them by the teacher. As we shall see in a later chapter, the sort of study habits which a

8   *Teenagers in an informal learning situation*

teacher plans for his pupils to acquire and develop, make important contributions to the quality of their mental processes in later years. The more that they are helped to find out for themselves, to suggest possible solutions to problems, to find similarities, relationships and explanations, the more successful will they be in their learning and the more skilled they will gradually become at using their intellectual processes in other situations. Of course, these activities can be undertaken only if the basic skills and information are already mastered by the learner and if the teacher gives guidance and builds up their confidence to make sure that they can succeed. A balance needs to be struck between learning methods which require them to remember information which they have been given and those which require them to use that information as well as their own imaginations to learn and to understand new situations.

How long and how much?

In addition to the general principles described above, there are some more specific considerations in planning learning activities. For example, how long should one activity last before changing to something else? The span of attention varies according to the pupils' age and maturity levels and according to the sort of learning activity required of them. Young children may need a change of activity and focus several times in a lesson whereas older ones are able to concentrate for a longer period of time. As a general rule, learning is more successful if it can be undertaken through a series of different activities, both because varied activity is itself an important contributor to learning and because a change of activity at the right time renews motivation and concentration. Experience will show you how long to expect your pupils to pay attention to one task but lesson planning should include a variety of activities, so that as soon as the pupils are no longer using their time constructively a change can be made.

Another consideration is how much content to expect the pupils to learn at one sitting. Again, this depends upon their age and ability as well as the nature of the material to be learned. Usually learning is more successful if, once they have understood the general purpose and scope of the whole topic or process, the pupils work on relatively limited aspects, each following on naturally from the previous part until all have been covered. Then it is essential that the whole be put together, having the effect of revising earlier parts, strengthening the links between them and forming a firm basis for further learning. This is why it is better at the beginning to plan a whole topic rather than isolated lessons.

In the last resort, although thorough preparation beforehand is essential, the teacher's sensitivity towards the pupils' reactions, difficulties and achievements and his willingness to change and modify his plans are the best enablers of learning, especially if the climate of the classroom is one of confidence and positive encouragement.

Summary

The important considerations to be made by a teacher in preparing for successful learning are:

1 *Who are the learners?*
their age, sex, general ability level
their present knowledge and skills
the topics and activities that interest them
the motives for learning that can be used
their usual attention span and the time of the day that the lessons
   timetabled for (i.e. how tired and hungry are the pupils likely to
   be?).

2 *What is the topic or skill to be learned?*
This should be stated in very specific terms as objectives (i.e. what should the pupils be able to do, or to do better, as a result of the learning which is being planned?).
For example, a map-making lesson for young children could be planned on the following basis:
   By the end of the lesson the children should be able to show on
   an outline plan of the classroom, given to them by the teacher,
   the relative position of the door, windows, chalk board and the
   teacher's table.
A domestic science lesson for older pupils could be something like this:
   By the end of the lesson the pupils should be able to identify,
   from a given list, those foods which are largely protein, those
   which are largely fat and those largely carbohydrate and write a
   sentence accurately describing the use to which the human
   body puts each food type.
Identifying the topic to be taught in this way, rather than baldly

stating something like 'Drawing plans', or 'Types of food and their function', takes you a long way towards preparation of the lesson itself, gives a clear indication of what you need to arrange for the learners to do, and exactly how you will assess their actual learning.

3 *What are the important parts of the topic or skill which make up the whole?*
Each step should lead from the previous one into the next one, in logical order.

In the first example in 2, the logical steps could be identified as something like this:
(i) some possible needs for a plan of the classroom;
(ii) the relative position of the doors and windows in the room itself;
(iii) the outline plan, ensuring that each child understands which line represent which wall;
(iv) how to show windows, doors and a table on a plan;
(v) ensure on a practice plan that each child understands what is to be done;
(vi) individuals draw their own doors, etc. on the given outline plan.

In the second example the steps could be something like this, depending on what the pupils already know about food groups and values:
(i) ensure that they know the consequences of a diet inadequate in fats, proteins and carbohydrates respectively;
(ii) source of each food group, especially those within their own environment and experience;
(iii) how to identify (in layman's terms) each food type;
(iv) common examples of each type.

Naturally in both cases there are other ways of identifying the steps and the objectives, depending largely upon how much of the important information and skill they already have.

4 *How will the overall objectives, the scope and the purpose of the topic be made clear to the pupils?*
This is to make sure that they see its purpose and know what is to be expected of them.

There are various ways in which this can be done, the most effective ones being those which make the children feel that they themselves *need* to know or do what is offered. In the first example, it might be enough to tell them that their parents would like to know what the classroom looks like and where to find their desk when they come to an open day. Putting in the doors, windows and teacher's desk is merely a start to help them later to put their own desk in the right place. In the second example, their own health may be of interest, or how to make the best use of very limited money or food resources. Some vivid points can be made in both these themes, by direct example, by discussing current issues in their own areas or countries, etc..

5 *What learning activities and assessment procedures will be used?*
These should be outlined for each sub-topic, to be planned in more detail when particular lessons or parts of lessons are being prepared.

6 *How will the whole topic or skill be put together once each sub-section has been mastered?*

7 *How will the achievement of the learning objectives, as stated in step 2, be tested?*

I hope that you will see that much of the thinking and planning needed to complete the preparation for successful learning which the final three headings suggest has already been done when considering the earlier headings. All that is necessary is for the teacher to organize his ideas into a practical plan and see that he has the necessary teaching materials ready.

Once the teacher knows his pupils well he will find that answering the points in step 1 can be completed quickly and need not be written out in full; a quick mental reminder is usually enough. Even successful, experienced teachers, however, find that the discipline of writing down the answers to the questions asked in the other steps makes successful learning more likely, especially if the details of learning activities are varied and selected to ensure that the learning objectives can be achieved. Once any part of the planned activity has been completed it will be necesssary to assess how successful it was and what additional work needs to be done by individuals and groups before the next sub-topic or skill is introduced. Similarly at the end of the series of lessons which make up the whole unit, the overall results will need to be analysed and difficulties identified so that further instruction and practice can be planned. Periodically, when it seems relevant, the learning achieved in the earlier parts of the overall topic can be referred to, to reinforce the understanding and the links which help to retain it in the learners' memories.

Application 12

1 Using the headings of the seven steps, plan at least two different topics or skills, preferably ones that you can reasonably expect to teach in the near future to a class with which you are familiar. Remember that the topic or skill may stretch over several timetabled periods.
2 At the earliest opportunity, teach at least one of your planned topics during a period of continuous teaching experience. Plan each sub-section of the topic in the light of what happened in the previous lesson. To do this you will need to keep a detailed record of achievement and problems which may arise.

If at all possible work with a fellow student, watching and constructively analysing each other's planning and teaching. It is hoped that a tutor will also be available for advice and discussion.

Further reading

Read the chapters on learning which appear in most educational psychology textbooks, several of which are likely to be on your library shelves.

For example, Vander Zanden, James W., *Educational Psychology in Theory and Practice*, New York, Random House, 1980, pp 122 to 178 and Sprinthall, R.C. and Sprinthall N.A., *Educational Psychology; a Developmental Approach*, Reading, Massachusetts, 1974, pp 189 to 249.

Examples of work in specific areas of learning are in:

Gay, J., and Cole, M., *The New Mathematics and Old Culture; a study of Learning among the Kpelle of Liberia*, New York, Holt, Rinehart and Winston, 1967, and

Cole, M., Gay, J. and Glick, P., 'Some experimental studies of Kpelle quantitative behaviour', in Berry, J., and Dasen P.R., (eds.) *Culture and Cognition*, London, Methuen, 1974, p 161.

There are likely to be many more which have resulted from research done in colleges and universities in your country. See how many you can find, and compare notes with fellow students.

CHAPTER SEVEN
More about how our thinking and learning abilities develop

Some necessary labels

Most teachers would agree that the most important aspect of their pupils' development is that of their ability to think and to learn. The terms which describe these processes are *intellectual* or *mental*, and include such activities as understanding, remembering, reasoning, solving problems and making decisions. Sometimes they are thought of as abilities which enable one to use what has been experienced and learned in the past in order to understand and decide how to act in the present, or even in the future. The centre of intellectual activity is the brain. The term used by psychologists for intellectual activities is *cognition*, which includes all the ways in which we come to know about and understand the world in which we live, to learn from it and to think about it.

We make contact with our environment and anything that happens in it through our senses, i.e. eyes, ears, tongue, skin, muscles and so on. These carry their information as electrical impulses which travel along certain nerve pathways in the body to the central nervous system, most of which is situated in the brain. There, the electrical signals are sorted out and given meaning, some being stored in our memories, others being rejected or used as the basis for further actions by the individual. Because our environments and experiences are special to ourselves there is a great deal of difference among individuals in the information from the senses which is processed and stored.

A teacher needs to have a sound knowledge of how his pupils' intellectual, or *cognitive* processes work in order to be able to use them to the best advantage. Firstly, he needs to know what intellectual skills to expect his pupils to have and how they are likely to change and mature as they grow older and gain more experience of school and their own environments. Secondly, he needs to know in what ways the intellectual abilities of his pupils are likely to differ from each other's. With this knowledge he will be better able to cater for individual differences, ensuring that each learner has the best opportunity to succeed in his learning. Thirdly, he needs to know as much as possible about the outside influences, environmental experiences and learning activities which can affect the development of efficient cognitive processes. Fourthly, he needs to know whether it is possible to measure the intellectual ability that his pupils possess, and, if it is, how to do it and how far he can rely on the results. Sound knowledge in these areas will have an important influence on how he approaches his work as a teacher.

Before we begin to discuss the topic of intellectual activity in more detail, there is another widely used term which needs clarifying. It is *intelligence*, which is not the same as *intellect*, (another term for the *mind*), nor is it the same as *cognition*, which refers to the activities of the *intellect* or the *mind*. Instead, it refers to how well the intellect and the cognitive processes work and suggests a comparison between the efficiency of one person's mental functioning and another's. Often there is an adjective attached to the word 'intelligence' ... such as 'high' or 'low', 'average' or 'above average', and so on ... which reinforces its use to compare the intellectual ability of some people with that of others. You have probably met the term *intelligence test*, about which there will be more later. These are tests which try to measure the actual, or the potential, mental quality of individuals so that one can get an idea of what to expect of them in their learning performance. Most intelligence tests give results which show how one individual's scores compare with those of others. In addition to the comparative aspect, the word 'intelligence' often suggests that people have a generalized capacity or overall quality when using their intellects. In other words, it suggests that one is capable of learning and understanding a wide range of different things at more or less the same level. As we shall see later, the situation is much more complicated than that.

Some changing beliefs about cognition

The story of the changing ideas and theories about the intellect and how it works is interesting and helps us to understand many present day educational ideas and practices, including those in Third World countries. For example, in the industrially developing northern hemisphere countries, when the establishment of universal primary education took place in the mid-nineteenth century, most of those involved with planning its provision, and most of the teachers then employed, believed that virtually all the pupils were capable of the same level of achievement. There was no science of psychology and very little scientific inverstigation of human abilities to give a different point of view. The educational aims of the publicly provided schooling were much more limited than they are today and the curriculum was mainly confined to teaching the pupils to read, write and do simple arithmetic. Of course, there were exceptions because there have always been gifted and sensitive teachers who do what they can personally to enrich the educational lives of their pupils. But in the eyes of the authorities, a successful teacher was one who brought all his pupils to a certain level of proficiency in the basic subjects. Failure by a pupil to achieve this level was usually thought to be the fault of the teacher, or laziness and lack of discipline on the part of the pupil. Indeed, at one time, and fortunately fairly briefly, teachers in England were paid according to the numbers of their 'successful' pupils.

Is intellectual ability inherited?

Advances in scientific method and knowledge made during the nineteenth century showed that among plants and animals there were individual differences for a vast array of traits and the theory of genetic inheritance was advanced to account for many of these. It soon became obvious that there was a strong link between parents and their offspring in many aspects of their appearance and development. When certain parent plants and animals were chosen, because they possessed particular traits, their offspring were very likely to inherit the traits and pass them on the their own offspring, in turn.

Investigation of some human physical traits, such as height, weight and the size of hands, feet, etc., showed that if one looked at the measurements for a large number of people from a similar background, the figures spread out in a regular pattern, most of them collecting round a mid-point and the rest spread evenly on either side. The pattern of measurements was so regular that it

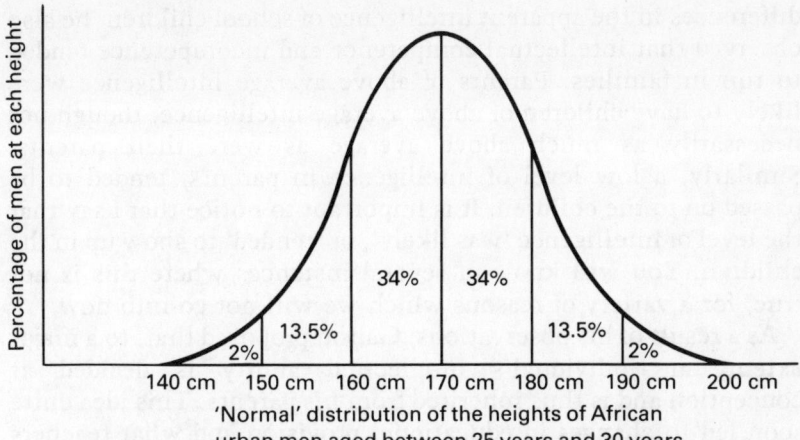

'Normal' distribution of the heights of African urban men aged between 25 years and 30 years.

was possible to tell in advance how many there would be at any point on the distribution. Such a spreading out of the figures made a curve rather like the one shown here, which shows what percentage of a population of urban African men, aged between 25 and 30, were at particular points in the height scale. If you measured the heights of all your fellow male students and plotted them in the same way, you would get a very similarly shaped curve, though the middle height and the tallest and shortest heights might be a little different. Similarly, if the heights of all the female students were measured, the distribution would take the same shape, though the actual measurements are likely to be lower. Such a pattern of distribution of traits which are mostly determined by genetic inheritance, as height is, is known as *normal distribution*, and it is an important idea which, as we shall see, has been and still is an influence in educational matters, especially when it is applied to the spread of intellectual capacity.

You will see that about 34% of such a group are likely to be between 160 cm and 170 cm tall, another 34% will be between 170 cm and 180 cm tall, with 170 cm being the average height. The rest of the men are spread out above and below these heights, as many being below as above.

The first person seriously to suggest that the individual differences in the ability to learn, think and reason which are common in schools, could be caused by inherited differences was an Englishman, Francis Galton, in the second half of the nineteenth century. He observed not only the fact of individual differences in the apparent intelligence of school children; he also observed that intellectual competence and incompetence tended to run in families. Parents of above average intelligence were likely to have children of above average intelligence, though not necessarily as much above average as were their parents. Similarly, a low level of intelligence in parents, tended to be passed on to the children. It is important to notice that I say that the level of intelligence 'was likely', or 'tended' to show up in the children. You will know of several instances where this is not true, for a variety of reasons which we will not go into now.

As a result of his observations, Galton proposed that, to a major extent, an individual's intellectual ability is decided at conception and is thus inherited from his parents. This idea quite soon led to changes in educational provision and what teachers could expect of their pupils. For example, it was realised that not all pupil failure was the fault of the teacher, or of the pupil's behaviour and efforts.

Galton took two more important steps in his thinking about, and experimenting in, the development of intellectual abilities. His arguments went rather like this:

(i) It is obvious that human intellectual ability is inherited and because of this it must, like other more easily measured traits such as height, be spread in the population on a *normal curve*. This means that it should be possible to calculate mathematically the percentages of the population which will have particular levels of intellectual ability. About 68% will measure close to the mid-point, the remaining 32% being evenly balanced above and below this, with very small numbers at each end.

(ii) Since we know (argued Galton) the proportions of the population likely to inherit intellectual capacity at various points in the range, it should be possible to find ways of measuring an individual's intellectual level. Tests, puzzles and tasks which can be successfully completed by the percentages of children, all of the same age, which appear at each point on a normal curve, are likely to be measuring the intellectual capacity of those children. A group of such puzzles and tasks all of which give the same results at a particular age level and which are more difficult for younger and easier for older children, can form an intelligence test which could give important information about an individual's quality of intellectual function and his ability to benefit from schooling.

This logical argument, as put forward by Galton, includes the suggestions that a generalized quality of intellectual function exists in any one individual and it is this which is being measured. Such a generalized aspect of intellectual activity later become known as 'g'. Galton also assumed that 'g' remains more or less the same throughout one's life. Its scope will widen gradually as one grows but one will always stay more or less in the same place on the scale of individual differences. A highly intelligent person will normally always score highly on intelligence tests, and so on across the distribution. A third assumption which Galton makes is that the quality of 'g', or general intellectual ability, is not influenced by learning opportunities and other educational experiences. Intelligence tests measure, it was thought, the inherited possibilities. As we shall see later, the story is not as simple as this, but for many years such an idea of the existence of an inherited potential intellectual quality and the possibility of measuring it, was widely held and greatly influenced the provision of schooling, educational assessment, selection and expectation. It is still an influential view, in many parts of the world, as we shall see later.

Measuring intellectual ability

The work and ideas of Francis Galton were built on by people such as Professors Binet and Simon who, in the early years of this century, were given the task of finding ways of identifying, as early as possible, those French school children who, because of low intellectual capacity, would be unlikely to benefit from normal schooling. For many years they worked on devising tests to measure intelligence, using Galton's ideas of normal distribution and of the existence in every individual of his own fairly unchanging intellectual capacity. The tests were collected into small groups, each group being suitable for children within an age range. This made it possible for any person's score on a series of tests to be compared with that of others of the same chronological age. Those who could do the tests intended for older children were said to have the *mental age* of those children and those who could complete only those tests intended for younger children were allocated the younger *mental age*. For example, a child of 10 years of age who could do tests which the average 12 year old could do was given a mental of age of 12, whereas one who could succeed only at the average eight year old's level was said to have a mental age (*MA* for short), of eight years.

A further, simple calculation proved to be even more useful than the mental age, because it allowed the ability of individuals to be compared with that of others regardless of their chronological age. It involved turning the mental age into a percentage score. Someone whose mental age was the same as his actual age, i.e. someone who was thought to have just average mental ability, was given a score of 100. An individual's mental age was worked out as a percentage of his chronological age, giving a figure ranging either above, below, or at, 100. For example, a child of 10 years of age who attained the same score as a 12 year old was said to have an intelligence score of 120, the calculation being done as follows:

$$\frac{\text{mental age (12 years)}}{\text{chronological age (10 years)}} \times \frac{100}{1}$$

i.e. $\frac{12}{10} \times \frac{100}{1} = 120$

The formula for this process is usually written $\frac{MA}{CA} \times \frac{100}{1}$

The technical name for the score produced in this way is *Intelligence Quotient*, abbreviated to *IQ*. As a further example, consider the child with a mental age of eight and a chronological age of ten years. Using the formula . . .

$$\frac{8}{10} \times \frac{100}{1} = 80 \ldots$$

he is said to have an IQ of 80, well below the average. Intelligence tests were usually constructed so that an individual's IQ stayed roughly the same throughout his life.

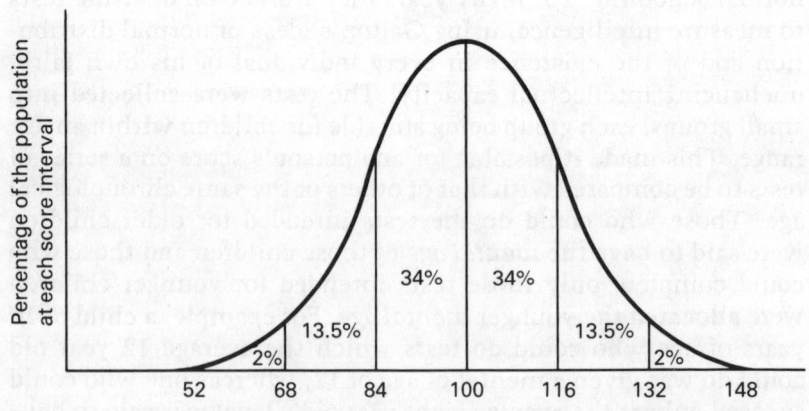

Distribution of scores of a population on intelligence tests

Going back to the idea of intellectual ability being largely inherited, the Binet-Simon, and most subsequently produced intelligence tests, give results which fit the curve of normal distribution. The usual divisions on the curve are at 16 IQ point intervals, as shown in the diagram.

You can see that a high proportion of the population is grouped round the average score, with much smaller numbers at either end, the remaining 1% are shared between the extremes of the scale, about half of them being severely mentally handicapped and the other half being the outstandingly intelligent.

Once an IQ is known, it becomes possible to compare an individual's potential intellectual ability with that of others who have been given the same test. One would expect someone scoring above 120 to be potentially able to achieve highly in their school learning. Similarly, someone with an IQ of less than 80 could be expected to have some learning problems in an ordinary classroom.

There is one further point to note, while reminding you that intelligence tests are made to fit a normal distribution curve, and do not themselves *prove* that intellectual ability is normally distributed. Binet and Simon, and many other test constructors included in their batteries of tests only those items which gave the same results for boys and girls. Tests which seemed to give different scores for each sex were rejected so that one cannot say that boys and girls have the same intellectual potential because they obtain the same test results. This may be so, but one cannot use the evidence of results of tests which were designed to avoid sex differences.

Since the work of Binet and Simon, many other tests of intelligence have been developed and the original ones refined and extended in many countries. The direct descendants of the original tests are still widely used today, though the results may be interpreted rather differently.

Some effects on education of a genetic view of intelligence

Before returning to the story of the development of our understanding of the intellect and cognitive processes, let us look at some of the important effects on education and teaching that the concepts described above could have. For example, if it is strongly believed that genetic inheritance is largely responsible for individual differences in intellectual ability and that such differences can be measured by tests, then one would expect to find an education system which has different sorts of education for different ability levels. Such a system would need a process of selection to sort the pupils into their ability groups, with the expectation that the teacher's job would be made easier by grouping together children of similar ability. Using the percentages of children falling at different places on the normal curve, the numbers of school places needed at each level could be calculated well in advance and the required numbers of teachers provided. Some older countries, notably Great Britain, did for a while make much of its educational provision on such a basis, especially at the post-primary level. For a number of years after the Second World War most eleven year old children were assessed both for attainment in basic subjects and on intelligence tests so that they could be allocated to an appropriate secondary school course. Roughly 30% were offered an academic grammar school place while most of the rest went on to a less academic secondary modern school. Most of those whose IQ's were considered to be too low for such schooling, were sent to special schools or classes while a few were considered not to be educable in schools at all. While such a rigid grading system is now considerably modified for reasons which will become clear later, in many countries the thinking behind it still subtly influences such things as educational selection, class streaming and public examination setting and marking. It is not, at present, being argued that these are necessarily bad practices, but it is important that educators are aware of the psychological beliefs that underlie them so that they can decide whether they are justifiable.

Further developments in understanding intellectual activities

In the past twenty years or so, psychologists have added important new ideas to our understanding of cognitive development. One of the most important of these is the realisation that a genetic explanation for individual differences in intellectual ability is not enough. For example, it was noticed that both measured IQ and success in school learning were often related to the social class and the educational and environmental opportunities that children had had. Studies of children who had not lived with their own parents but had been adopted into homes of people of different background showed that such children were often nearer in ability level to their adoptive parents than their own natural ones. Then, too, children brought up in very limited environments, such as in certain Middle East orphanages (now much improved), all appeared to be of very low intelligence, which could not be accounted for genetically. A fast-increasing quantity of evidence, more of which you can read about for yourself (see the end of this chapter), pointed to the conclusion that things other than just genetic inheritance are responsible for the intellectual ability that one develops. It also suggests that one must be very cautious about accepting the score on an intelligence test as a true indication of an individual's intellectual potential. The present, widely but not universally, accepted view is that while one's genetic contribution probably does decide the sort of intellectual capacity that one *could* develop if all the circumstances were ideal, the extent to which this inborn potential develops and becomes usable depends on the sort of intellectual activities and stimulation that the individual's home, school and social environment provides.

Philip Vernon proposed that it would be useful to think of intelligence in two main ways. Firstly, there is Intelligence 'A', which he says represents the possible development as decided at conception. It used to be thought that intelligence tests could measure this directly with a high degree of accuracy, but this is now known not to be so. Intelligence 'B' is the label he gives to the actual intellectual abilities which have been developed for use by the individual. It is not the same as Intelligence 'A', and we can only guess about 'A' from studying 'B'. A good, intellectually-stimulating environment could make more of the potential ability. Vernon later added a third label, Intelligence 'C', which is a useful way of thinking about the score in an intelligence test. This figure is obtained by sampling some of the things which the individual can do using his Intelligence 'B'. It is likely that it is a fair reflection of his actual ability but it could happen that, by chance, the samples are not typical of the way his intellect works, so a misleading result could be obtained.

Further considerations in understanding intellectual abilities

As observation and research into the development of intellectual abilities expanded it soon became obvious that the beliefs on which Galton, Binet and the many others working along the same lines based their conclusions, were not sufficient to explain the many exceptions that have subsequently been found. For example, you will remember that intelligence tests were thought to measure inherited potential ability as well as to give a picture of a steady expansion in the scope of mental capacity up to adolescence. Despite this, test scores for some children, especially those who had experienced important changes in their environmental circumstances, often changed considerably at different stages of their lives. One can only conclude that the tests were measuring aspects of their ability other than their inherited potential.

More importantly, there was a growing body of evidence which suggested that an individual's ability to make sense of, and to use, the information coming to him through his senses from the outside world did more than merely expand in scope with age. Just as various aspects of physical function (e.g. full sexual function) mature over the years until full capacity is attained, so, it was thought, do one's cognitive abilities. They are not merely more efficient as time passes; they are different in their nature and in the activities that they can perform. The most important name in this aspect of our understanding of cognitive development is Jean Piaget, a Swiss biologist whose ultimate aim was to construct a comprehensive explanation of how we come to know and understand the world about us when our only direct contact with it is through our senses (sight, touch, taste, smell, sound, temperature, etc.). It is important to remember at this point that many of Piaget's ideas developed from his own observations which he interpreted in the light of his knowledge of how plants and animals grow and develop. Much of his work is difficult to test scientifically for oneself, although a great deal of research has grown out of it.

His main proposals arising from his observations and interpretations are as follows:
(i) Because we are not born with direct knowledge of our environments (i.e. everything that is outside ourselves, including even our own bodies), we must somehow make a sort of mental picture, or, better still, a mental 'model' of what the information from our senses suggests to us. To do this we have to use a variety of mental processes so that we can remember past experiences, compare them with new ones, organize them logically in our minds so that they make sense and can be used to help us to

understand and react appropriately to new experiences. Thus, says Piaget, human beings do not just take in new experiences passively but usually actively explore them and make them part of their mental equipment, though there are times when new facts or experiences are rejected.

(ii) Because every individual's experience is *never* exactly the same as that of anyone else, everyone's mental 'model' must be to some extent different from everyone else's. People from similar backgrounds, cultures, etc., are likely to have mental models which overlap with each other's so that we can usually communicate fairly sensibly. Later we shall explore important educational implications of this point.

(iii) Since human beings are part of a continuity of living things, from the simplest single celled creature, and since Nature is very reluctant to introduce new mechanisms and techniques when existing ones can be adapted, some of the basic processes by which they interact with their environments are found in all living things. In order to survive, even simple creatures can adapt themselves to their environments or adapt their environments to themselves, or both. All living things need to keep in balance with their surroundings; Piaget uses the word *equilibrium*. For example, a creature in need of food will seek it and take it into his body, which digests the essential parts and gets rid of the rest. It has *accommodated* itself in order to find, take in and digest the food, and *assimilated* it into its body, having now achieved, at least for a short while, *equilibrium*. This is a simple basic example of what Piaget says is the main motivator for all action. Human beings use the same *Functional Invariants* of *accommodation* and *assimilation* to construct their personal 'mental models' of their own environments, and are motivated by the same thing, i.e. the need to feel comfortably in balance. New experiences may not appear to fit in with what he already 'knows' so that the individual will work on both the new and the old knowledge, modifying one or the other, or both, until they fit neatly together into, what is for him, a more logical 'model'. This, too, has important implications for the learning process which we shall discuss further later.

(iv) The cognitive skills which are available to the growing individual are not there in their final complete form at birth but gradually develop in function as he matures physically. It follows that the 'mental model' of a child's own world is limited, not only by his experience but also by the thinking skills that he can use when sorting out and making sense of his experiences. Piaget identifies four major stages in the development of cognitive processes, each one growing out of the previous one though we continue to use the earlier abilities as well when necessary. He suggests average ages at which each new stage is likely to begin to be reached, but great care must be taken not to use the ages as anything more than a very rough guide. One must also take care not to think of the change from one stage of thinking to the next as being a sudden jump. The developmental processes go on continuously, greater and greater complexity being added as they progress.

Piaget at first suggested that the progressive development probably happened naturally, in obedience to the inherited instructions of the genes. He soon became convinced, however, that although the order in which new cognitive abilities matured was the same for all normal people, the age at which they developed and the their efficiency with which they could be used, varied considerably. Some of the variation could be explained by an individual's probable Intelligence 'A', or his inherited possibilities. But much of it seemed to be related to the sorts of learning experiences he had had and the requirements arising from his environment. Here again, you can see important implications for education, which will be discussed more fully later.

The stages of cognitive development proposed by Piaget are:

(i) The *sensori-motor*, which is the main one up to about two years of age. During this period, the baby gradually comes to make sense of his environment by building up from his experiences a personal 'model' of it. But his thinking abilities, at this stage, are mostly in the form of sensations, movements and feelings. He does not yet have any real language to help him think about and make sense of things and events. So his mental 'model' is likely to be in the form of shapes, movements, sounds, textures, tastes, scents and so on, a concept which is difficult for us to understand. As new experiences occur which are not already in his 'model' he changes it mentally to accommodate them. Gradually, as his nervous system matures and his senses receive more information from the world around him, his 'model' becomes closer to his own real world and a sound basis on which to develop further understanding.

Piaget says that for much of the time during this stage the baby does not see himself as being separate from his surroundings. To him, they, and even other people, are all parts of himself. It is only later that he develops the idea that things and other people have an existence of their own which continues even when he is not there.

It is important to remember that all of us continue to use sensori-motor intelligence to enable us to act successfully in many situations. Many of the physical skills that we possess, such as throwing a ball, sewing, writing and driving a car, are a basic part of us and apparently remembered in the nerves and muscles rather than in the intellectual part of the brain. This means that we can use our thought processes to concentrate on *what* we are writing or sewing, *where* we throw the ball or *how* to manoeuvre the car safetly in the direction that we want.

(ii) The *pre-operational* stage, which begins to develop well before the sensori-motor-dominated one is over. At this time, the young child gradually becomes able to use mental pictures and images in place of sensations in his mental 'model'. This means that it becomes increasingly centred in his mind rather than in the muscles and sensory organs. He is also learning a verbal language, a process which proceeds rapidly, so that he can soon use words as symbols in his model of his world. These begin to replace sensations and images, which are rather clumsy when used to think with. Verbal symbols allow him to think much more flexibly and to understand more complex ideas, which in turn enable even more learning and intellectual development to take place.

Even though the pre-operational stage, roughly from about two years to six or seven in most children, is a time when a great deal of very important learning takes place, Piaget says that the sorts of thinking and understanding which children are capable of is limited because they cannot deal with more than one aspect of an experience at a time. This means that they may not be able to see the relationship between two separate ideas. One typical way in which he demonstrated his point was to show two identical balls of clay to children up to the age of about seven years. As soon as they had agreed that the balls were exactly the same as each other he rolled one of the balls into a sausage shape and asked the children whether there was more clay in the ball or in the sausage. Younger children tended to insist that there was now more clay in the sausage than in the ball. Piaget said that this indicated that they could deal only with one feature of the clay at a time, in this case the length. They could not think of the total amount of clay as being independent of the shape into which it was moulded. Certainly this reaction of young children is very widely found, though other explanations than Piaget's are possible. It has been suggested, for example, that lack of experience and an insufficient understanding of the words 'more than' may be the cause of the error. Probably there is some truth in both explanations.

The label *pre-operational*, given by Piaget to this stage of intellectual development, reflects what he sees to be a period when the average child is unable to use logical operations to enable him to make sense of his experiences and fit them into his mental 'model'. This, says Paiget, is because the brain and the central nervous system are not yet fully mature. He can still deal only with what he experiences directly, and then only as a series of separate facts or observations.

(iii) The *concrete operational* stage, which usually begins to develop somewhere between five and seven years of age. According to Piaget the maturing brain and nervous system gradually allow children to be able to think about (i.e. *operate* on) more than one aspect of an experience at a time. This means that they can develop an even more realistic and useful mental model, and a richer understanding of themselves and their environments. Children who are moving beyond the pre-operational stage are now able to accept that changing the shape of the clay ball has not changed the amount of clay that is there. They are better able to use language to describe and discuss ideas with others.

This new ability has an important part to play in school learning. In arithmetic, for example, a pre-operational child would not be able to understand that a number, such as 12, is made up not only of 12 separate items but can also be four groups of three items, or two groups of six items, or ten plus two more. Once he is mentally capable of thinking of the number 12 as being something which stays the same no matter how each single item within it is rearranged, he is said to be able to *operate* logically with the number 12. He has attained the *concept* of the number 12, or, as in the case of the clay balls, a *concept* of a quantity, which is independent of its shape. Before he has attained the concept of 12, he might be able to learn to chant the multiplication table of numbers involving 12, or do mechanical sums which include it. But he will not really understand what he is doing; he will instead be following a set of rules which he has learned, almost as if it were a magic spell.

Another example to illustrate the difference between pre-operational and operational thinking is in family relationships. For example, until he is sufficiently mentally mature a child will not be able to understand that his mother is someone different in relation to other people. She is someone's daughter, sister, wife, aunt, friend, teacher, etc. The author experienced this when one of her own children was about five years old. She told him that she was going to teach at a nearby college for a few hours a week, while he was at school. Anxiously he asked, 'Will you still be my mummy?'. Fortunately he accepted the reassurance, especially once he found that she was there whenever he came home. Concepts such as these are complex, and to understand and to be able to use them requires both the opportunity to learn them but also the cognitive maturity to see the relationships between the parts and the whole.

So far we have ignored the word 'concrete' which is part of the name given to this stage of cognitive development. Piaget suggests that for several years, and at least until he reaches adolescence or young adulthood, a child still has an important limitation to his thinking and ability to understand. Even though he is able to use adult logic and understand relationships, he is unlikely to be able to understand and think about ideas which cannot be first understood in practical ways. It seems as though the child has to learn as much as possible through practical experience, preferably directly, though it can be achieved through realistic descriptions, illustrations and demonstrations. In other words he needs to have 'concrete' or real experience through which he can develop and enrich his concepts. He cannot, says Piaget, really understand and think about non-concrete ideas such as honesty, democracy, climate, religion, algebraic mathematics and so on. He can often, of course, apparently use the words correctly. He can identify situations which are honest or dishonest, his meaning of the word being dependent on his own experience of judgements of others of honesty and dishonesty. He can take part in class elections, and see them as part of the democratic process, but he is unlikely to have a concept of the abstract term 'democracy'. Piaget says that while the child in this concrete operational stage of development can operate logically with ideas which have a direct meaning for him because they can be presented to him in ways which are direct and realistic, he cannot yet deal mentally with ideas experienced less directly.

From the earliest age, children learn quite a lot from trying out their ideas and explanations for things on other people, or by practical experiment. When their ideas seem to fit the real situation they accept them and use them again. For example, a child who is learning to talk makes many mistakes, at least some of which are the result of wrong guesses about the rules of grammar. He may say 'runned' instead of 'ran', because he has noticed that many words form the past tense by adding 'ed'... stop/stopped, crash/crashed. It can be said that he unconsciously forms a *hypothesis* (i.e. a sensible guess at a rule, or at what will happen if he does certain things) and then tests out that hypothesis to see if he is right. If not, he usually tries to find another hypothesis until he gets one which does seem to fit the facts. In the pre-operational stage he seems to form a hypothesis which involves only one aspect of a situation. Once he is able to use concrete operational thinking he can form complex hypotheses about experiences and happenings but is limited to practically-testable ideas arising from direct experience. True scientific investigation in which ideas go beyond the direct and practical is not yet possible to any extent, in Piaget's view.

As with the previously described Piagetian stages, the child's intellectual skills gradually mature and throughout the several years during which this is happening he is constructing an ever more complex and flexible internal 'model' which is made up of the knowledge, skills, concepts and ideas that he has learned. The richer this is the better it is as a basis from which to absorb still more knowledge and understanding, and from which to make decisions about how to think and act. The educational implications of Piaget's ideas will be discussed later, once we have looked at his final stage in cognitive development.

(iv) The *formal operational*, which Piaget suggested becomes possible from early adolescence. A young person at this stage, while still using the earlier cognitive methods, becomes increasingly able to identify general principles and rules from the range of practical experiences he has had. Soon he may become able to reason using these principles rather than having to think about specific and practical examples of them. He can now deal with the *form* of reasoning (hence the term formal operations) and can think about a wider range of concepts. For example, in agricultural science he becomes able to predict the likely success of selected crops in a certain area because he is able to reason with the principles which he has derived from his knowledge of the soil, climate, altitude and the nutritional needs of the crops. Such knowledge, combined with an understanding of likely markets, transport routes and their costs, etc., can be combined to help him make intelligent decisions which will lead to successful farming. This example illustrates well the need both to understand the abstract principles involved and to have accurate factual knowledge of the specific situation in which the principles have to be applied.

It must be remembered that the ability to use formal operational resoning does not necessarily lead to correct conclusions. The principles may be derived from inadequate experience, or from such sources as folklore and superstition. However, a person who is sufficiently mentally mature to be able to reason at the formal operational level is less likely than most people to be influenced by superstitions and non-reasoned arguments.

Piaget suggested that by no means everyone becomes able to use this higher level of intellectual activity. Almost no one uses it consistently, concrete experiences and concrete operational methods still being important, both to improve the knowledge from which new principles can be abstracted and to enable one to deal with new and immediate situations. There is evidence to suggest that the intellectual environment, home, school and community, and the sort of cognitive skills demanded by it, encourage or discourage the development of formal operational reasoning. Then, too, there is evidence to suggest that, especially among the intellectually more able children in a stimulating home and school environment, the ability to identify general principles and to test, predict and reason with them, begins to develop much earlier than adolescence. It is certain that there are wide individual and group differences in the levels of reasoning skills among adolescents and adults; it is possible that as many as 70% of people rarely, if ever, achieve any real competence in, or habitually use, the most advanced levels of reasoning.

Before looking at the educational implications of Piaget's arguments and observations about cognitive development and those of others who have tested and refined them, we should complete the story of the changing ideas about intellectual abilities and how they are influenced. For instance, you will remember that a widely held view of intellectual ability was that it was a generalized quality which seemed to affect all aspects of learning. Intelligence tests were designed to assess this general capacity, given the name 'g'. Later the existence of specific abilities, such as verbal and mechanical, were assumed, contributing in various proportions to certain tasks. Although Piaget was not concerned with the concepts of potential and real ability, he did accept that 'g' played an important part in determining how well the reasoning skills developed, accounting for at least some of the differences between individuals.

Recent thinking about intellectual functioning has tended to focus on individual differences in other sorts of thinking. For example, Guilford and others proposed that there are individual differences in the ability to think imaginatively and creatively. They suggest that such abilities are probably inherited to some extent and so likely to be spread in a population along a Normal Distribution dimension. A more accurate term for creative and imaginative thinking is *divergent thinking*, because it allows for unusual but logical conclusions to be drawn, or new and unusual ways of finding connections between them. A capacity to think divergently is necessary if there are to be new and inventive ideas. The opposite way of thinking is called *convergent* because the ideas and observations made are drawn together into one obvious conclusion. Evidence suggests that while most of us can use both sorts of thinking, especially when we are young, most people tend to prefer one or the other way of thinking. It seems that some environments and educational practices favour one rather than the other, convergent thinking being the most often found. The main reason for this is that most families and communities need their members to see things in the same way and to conform to tradition. Really divergent individuals, while being essential for progress and invention, are often difficult for the ordinary person to understand and manage, and can even seem to be a threat to the community in which they live. Schools, too, tend to favour convergers, especially those schools which are very concerned with ensuring that their pupils learn a set body of knowledge which is tested by traditional examinations. Unexpected and unusual ideas and solutions to problems are often not encouraged. The result is that there is often a serious lack of opportunity for children in school to develop their divergent and creative abilities since even a high degree of inherited potential ability needs to be properly used if it is to grow fully.

Another important intellectual ability which is thought to have an inherited basis but which needs environmental opportunities to develop fully is known as *spatial reasoning*. This is the ability to think about, understand and mentally manipulate diagrams, spaces and shapes; this is in contrast to verbal reasoning in which the use of language is essential. Such a mental ability is used in, for example, advanced mathematics, and much science, as well as in understanding and making maps, plans, diagrams and machine drawings. A wide range of individual differences in this ability is found among all groups. In addition, in many cultures, boys tend to become more competent at spatial reasoning and their related abilities than girls. The best of the girls are as good as the best of the boys, and the worst of the boys as bad as the worst of the girls but the average level of ability of boys is usually higher than that of girls.

The author investigated one aspect of spatial reasoning ability among Zimbabwean secondary school children, comparing the scores of rural and urban boys and rural and urban girls. They were tested at the beginning of the secondary school and again two years later, (i.e. at 13 and 15 years respectively). At 13 years, urban and rural boys scored very similarly, their scores following a more or less 'normal distribution'. On the other hand the average score of the girls was noticeably lower than that of the boys, with rural girls being a little better than urban girls.

Two years later the urban boys had improved, being better, on the average, than the rural boys. The girls had made almost no improvement in the ease with which they could do the spatial reasoning tests, though the rural ones retained their slight advantage.

These results can at least in part be explained in terms of environmental experience and expectations. Both rural and urban girls almost from their earliest years had had less freedom to move about and explore their surroundings than had the boys. But rural girls had probably been more actively involved in domestic and agricultural matters, using tools and household equipment more than their urban counterparts. At adolescence boys, especially urban boys, are increasingly involved in a mechanical and technical environment and may be expected to improve their spatial abilities more consistently than do rural boys. Urban girls are probably more limited in their scope outside the home and school than are rural ones who are protected by the extended family system and have more freedom to move within it. One must, of course, remember that research such as that just described deals with *average* scores. Within that there are wide individual differences and one must be careful not to make judgements about an individual without more information about him or her.

Exceptions to this finding exist in the few cultures in which boys and girls are treated exactly alike, especially in their toys, the games that they play and in the sort of family responsibilities that they carry. Examples of this have been found among a few Canadian Eskimo tribes. In such instances, the spatial abilities of girls are much closer to those of boys. Then, too, children, both boys and girls, whose early upbringing prevented them from moving about and exploring their surroundings, resulting in a limitation of their sensori-motor experience, are likely to have underdeveloped spatial abilities. This is particularly noticeable in cultures in which baby care practice includes keeping an infant for much of the day on his mother's back. He gains other important benefits but, when it is combined, as it often is, with a traditionally verbally based and bookish education system, both boys and girls can be handicapped in their ability to reason spatially.

This phenomenon has been a cause of concern in some Third World countries when technical colleges and certain university departments have found that many otherwise very able students have difficulty making practical interpretations of charts, maps, diagrams and plans. Hopeful results are emerging from special remedial courses and from school teaching methods which involve practical work of this nature. The extension of playgroups and other forms of pre-school educational also gives cause for optimisim.

Summary of the discussion so far

The general state of thinking about the factors which influence the development and use of intellectual abilities may be summarised as follows.

1 Although the potential limits to the intellectual abilities that an individual *could* develop are probably decided genetically at conception, the actual extent to which they are developed and become usable is probably much influenced by his own opportunities and experiences. These opportunities and experiences include:
a) his family, its attitudes, its interactions, its economic and educational circumstances and its habits and customs;
b) the community in which his family lives, its customs, attitudes and beliefs and its physical and technical circumstances;
c) his school, its educational aims and assessment procedures, its learning/teaching methods and attitudes towards uniformity and individuality;

2 Intellectual abilities probably include a generalized capacity which underlies all learning activities plus a number of fairly specialised activities. The potential for the latter is probably genetically determined but their development for use is probably dependent to some extent on the value which the family, community and education system place upon them. The most important of these for our purpose are the creative, verbal and spatial, or mechanical, though there are probably others as well.

3 The way in which we come to know and understand our own surroundings and the events in them is dependent, not only on the in-born potential intellectual capacity, but also on the gradual and orderly maturing of increasingly complex logical processes. The pattern of cognitive growth seems to be universal but the rate of progress and its effectiveness depend both on genetic potential and the opportunities to use and to improve each thinking skill. Home, community and school all have important parts to play in deciding how we can use the intellectual abilities which we inherit through our parents.

Application 13

Study the structure of the school system in which you are likely to work. Find out especially what provision there is made for children of different abilities. For instance, is there ability streaming in the classes? Is there any form of ability selection into secondary school and, if so, what form does it take? Is there provision either in special classes or schools for those who have, or seem to have, particular learning problems?

In all cases try to examine the ways in which the selection into different streams or schools is made. Is there any attempt to measure intelligence or what is often called 'scholastic aptitude', i.e. the ability to learn rather than what has actually been learned?

Discuss with your tutor and fellow students how far the selection is done by assessing what a pupil is capable of doing rather than on his achievement. Try to decide whether there is a generally held belief that the abilities and disabilities that the pupils show are mostly born in them. What you should try to do is to discover whether genetic inheritance, or educational experience or poor self-discipline, etc. are seen to be factors in educational progress, accounting for much of the observed individual differences.

Further reading

Your reading for this chapter should concentrate as far as possible on identifying the circumstances likely to be relevant to your own. The following are good sources

1 Wagner, D.A. and Stevenson, H.W., (eds.), *Cultural Perspectives on Child Development*, San Franciso, W.H. Freeman and Company, 1982, especially pp. 146 to 165, 167 to 180 and 182 to 207.
2 Berry, J. and Dasen, P.R. (eds.), *Culture and Cognition*, London, Methuen, 1974, especially the papers by Nyiti, (p. 146), Witkin,

(p. 99), Cole and Bruner, (p. 231), Wober, (p. 261) and Bovet, (p. 311).
3   Ashley Montague (ed.), *Race and IQ*, New York, Oxford University Press, 1975, especially the papers by Kagan, (p. 53), Bronfenbrenner and Ashley Montague, (p. 115), Bronfenbrenner, (p. 286) and Sanday (p. 220).

CHAPTER EIGHT

Some ways in which ideas about thinking and learning can influence educational methods and provision

In the last chapter, it was shown that human intellectual abilities and how they are used are very flexible so that they can be influenced by almost every aspect of an individual's life experience. We cannot say exactly how this happens, though work with animals such as rats, cats, dogs and monkeys suggests that the actual structure of the material making up the brain and central nervous system may become more fully developed if they live in an active and stimulating environment which ensures that they have to think about and learn from it. Of course, one must be cautious about drawing too many conclusions about human beings from animal behaviour. However, it seems reasonable to draw a parallel between the active and efficient brain of a healthy animal which has lived an interesting life in an exciting environment, and that of a child who has had a wealth of opportunities to explore, experiment and communicate with others while feeling safe and well-loved. The beneficial influence is greatest when the opportunities and experiences are organized and graded to suit the child's level of competence and development. An environment in which too little happens may handicap him, as might one in which too much happens too quickly and in a disorderly way, overwhelming him and making him withdraw.

The main implications, for the teacher, are, firstly that he must take into account the previous home, community and school experience of his pupils in order to get clues as to how to ensure

111

that they learn successfully. Secondly, he needs to ensure that the learning activities which he plans for his pupils give them opportunities to use and improve their creative, imaginative, spatial and verbal reasoning abilities, all of which seem to be capable of being improved or held back by the sort of use made of them. Thirdly, he must not only suit his teaching methods to the stage of mental development, as described by Piaget, that they are likely to have reached, but he must also see that they have every opportunity to take that development even further. Fourthly, he needs to make sure that what he expects them to learn to do or to know is organized and presented by him logically so that it can be linked easily to the learner's present understanding and make a firm basis from which further learning can take place. Fifthly, he must be cautious in his use of both attainment and standardised ability tests to assess his pupils' learning abilities, both as they are at present and how they may develop in the future. Intelligent behaviour is that which ensures that an individual learns and uses what he has learned to help him adapt his behaviour in new situations and solve future problems. The teacher's job is to make his pupils as 'intelligent' as it is possible for them to become, not just by making sure that they learn the skills and knowledge that are contained in the curriculum and syllabuses but by developing their mental processes in the wider sense. This applies equally to those whose natural intellectual gifts may be limited and to those who have great potential; their end levels will probably be different but the purposes of the educational process will be the same.

Particular considerations for Third World countries

As has been suggested often in this book, human needs and the principles of human development are common to almost all peoples but, because human abilities tend to develop in different ways in different circumstances, it is important for teachers to plan their work in the light of real knowledge of the actual circumstances of his pupils.

There is every indication that there is no overall superiority or inferiority of intellectual potential in any major group of people in the world. On the other hand, some special mental skills, such as spatial and mechanical reasoning, and creative and imaginative thinking, seem to develop better in some environments than in others. People in Third World and multi-cultural countries, at present, tend to show a wider variation in the development of some of these abilities. For example, the distribution of spatial reasoning abilities and mechanical and technical competence in countries where mechanical technology is relatively new and the cultural emphasis has been on verbal learning has already been mentioned.

Dawson gave tests, which are thought to assess the ability of people to think spatially and to identify the separate shapes which are included in complex diagrams, to two contrasting groups of people in Sierra Leone. The Temne at that time tended to bring their children up very strictly, often physically punishing them if they did not accept adult authority unquestiongingly. The mother was usually the dominant person in disciplining the children, the father seeming to be a background figure. The Mende, in contrast, brought their children up more permissively, with very little severe punishment, giving them real responsibility at an early age. The mother was a less dominant person in the upbringing of the children. The Mende, on the average, were better able to use the cognitive skills which were being measured.

Berry extended this research, adding other groups from contrasting environments, including Eskimos from the harsh Arctic, Australian Aborigines, and people from New Guinea. Within each group he compared the scores of those from rural-traditional and from urban-transitional environments (i.e. those who were undergoing fairly rapid economic and industrial change). There were differences between the ethnic groups themselves, mostly explicable by examining their environments. More important for teachers, is the fact that there were noticeable improvements among those who were moving into an environment with more demand for such intellectual skills.

Cole, Gay and Glick thought that perhaps some problems in spatial reasoning could be the result of there being no word in the language which had a sufficiently specific meaning for certain basic geometric shapes. For example, the Kpelle of Liberia used a word for a triangle which was also used to describe the shape of a tortoise shell, a bird's nest and a bow, none of which is a triangle in the sense that there are three straight sides meeting each other at an angle. He compared the spatial and geometric understanding of tribal adults, school children and illiterate children. The Kpelle school children had the highest level of geometric understanding, not different from that shown by United States children. On the other hand even unschooled Kpelle and others had no difficulty in making the practical measurements and assessments that they used in their everyday lives, as in measuring out quantities of rice. One must be very careful not to suggest that there is anything primitive about the abilities of people whose practical needs have not included the use of abstract concepts about shape, spatial relationships, mathematical thinking, etc. The evidence is strong that a people develops the intellectual skills that its environment requires and when the needs change, new skills will eventually develop.

On the other hand teachers must not ignore the possibility of their pupils having particular difficulties in certain intellectual skills and concepts because of their environmental experiences. Special attention needs to be paid to possible shortcomings which can best be identified by those living among and studying the real strengths and weaknesses in their cultural setting. Children need to be taught to use the less well-developed skills, which has important implications for the teaching methods adopted.

Many Third World countries which are rapidly becoming industrialised and dependent on twentieth century technology have found what is likely to be a temporary though important difficulty in training enough technicians and engineers, partly because of the restricted development of spatial and mechanical abilities in some of the population. The commonly found lack of ability among girls in this sphere has already been mentioned. Pre-school educational provision and teaching methods which involve pupils of all ages in practical exploration and manipulation of space, e.g. making and using maps, plans, diagrams and models, are likely to make good any underdevelopment while in themselves are valuable aids to efficient learning.

Some groups of adults in Third World countries, especially those whose upbringing was in rural areas, far from contact with books, pictures and industrialised areas, and whose schooling, if any, gave a very limited opportunity for learning to understand pictures, posters and book illustrations, have had difficulty in making sense of pictorial material. Research by such people as Deregowski in Zambia and Ethiopia, and by Jahoda and McGurk in Zimbabwe tended to show that experience of pictorial material from an early age helped to develop the ability to understand and interpret pictures in children. While all normal people would eventually become fairly proficient, children who had been to school were often more competent than their parents, especially when the latter had had only little experience of illustrated material. Here again, teachers in Third World countries will need to ask themselves whether any of their pupils from such backgrounds have similar difficulties. If so, a particular effort needs to be made from the earliest years to give pictorial experience.

Cultural differences also exist in the proportion of the population able and willing to think divergently and creatively, especially in the post-primary years. There is some evidence that people from traditionally conservative groups, whose way of life has not changed much for generations, are less likely to be imaginative and independent in their thinking and ideas than those from more open and challenging backgrounds. Teaching aims and practices can reinforce either the conservatism or the originality and independence of thought, the classroom teacher being very important in the process. Teaching methods which require the learners, wherever possible, to use their imaginations and which give them confidence to put forward and to defend their own independent points of view will encourage more flexible habits of thinking. In addition, it is important that, when testing pupils to see how well they have learned, the teacher should consider how to bring out and give credit for independence of ideas. If tests and examinations which determine how well the pupils have learned, ask only for straightforward and factual answers, then the development of the ability to express their own ideas could be handicapped. Incidentally, you have, I hope, noticed that teaching methods mentioned above are also those which we have already seen are most likely to lead to successful and long lasting learning.

The approach to cognitive development put forward by Piaget, Bruner and others has led to a large amount of research into the effects, if any, that different cultures and customs may have on the order in which cognitive abilities develop and in the rate of that development. As has been mentioned before, there seems to be a universal order of development but a noticeable variation in the average age at which the successive stages are reached, and the proportions of the population which achieve full competence. This is especially noticeable as the formal operation level. While the general environment is important in this development, schooling itself and the closeness with which teaching methods are linked to developmental levels and designed to improve them, can have an important effect. For example, Scribner and Cole studying the Vai in Liberia found that children who had become literate in an ordinary school were more likely to use Piaget's higher levels of reasoning than did those whose literacy was acquired in a Koranic school, possibly because of the emphasis on memorisation rather than more active learning methods used in the latter schools. A similar finding was made by Greenfield and others in West Africa among the Wolof in the Gambia. Schooled rural children were more able to do tests involving concrete and formal operational thinking than were unschooled rural children, or many adults. Urban Wolof children seemed less competent than rural ones at that time, perhaps because of the extensive use of the local simplified language in the town which may have been a less flexible basis for thinking about ideas.

Education in Third World countries has a particularly important role to play here, because of the strong possibility that a high proportion of children come from home environments which lack the opportunities for the full development of the cognitive abilities needed in their rapidly changing world. Even in longer established countries, differences in the average development of formal operational reasoning ability have been found between children from different schools in the same system. Those who attend schools which encourage originality, experiment, argument and a wide range of intellectual and practical activities are often superior to those who attend traditional, bookish and unadventurous schools.

No chapter on cognitive development would be complete without a comment of the place of language in it. Language offers a way of being able to refer to and think about things and ideas without having to have the real thing or a picture of it in front of one. The better the language development is, the more chance there is of efficient thinking and communication being developed. New experience links up with previous experience and knowledge to form a richer network of ideas which, in turn, adds still more value to the language. For example, a very young child hears the word 'dog' and soon uses it to refer to a dog which is well known to him. He then, as he hears the word used in different situations, realizes that there is a group of creatures called 'dog'. At first he may use the word to refer to any four-legged animal but soon his experience helps him to decide what particular attributes make the label 'dog' correct. Over the years, he widens his experience of dogs and the knowledge he gains makes him able to use the word with complete accuracy for a wide range of very different looking dogs. This is a simple illustration of how language and ideas help each other to develop. It applies to abstract just as much as to concrete ideas and events. The wider the individual's experience and the greater the opportunities he has to turn his practical experience into language, and to share it with others, the better he will be able to think and reason. One can see, then, that for all children language development is one of the most important aspects of education, especially when it is closely tied to their own experience. All teachers carry a heavy responsibility for developing the language skills of their pupils, which must involve much more than just expecting them to listen to the teacher talking, or to answer a few questions in class. It must also involve them in putting their own ideas into words, telling other people about them, explaining and discussing.

In addition, teachers must make sure that their pupils really understand important words which are needed for learning new ideas. Often people seem to use words correctly and to understand the concepts that they stand for but in fact their understanding is superficial or even inaccurate. There is need for a wide range of examples and illustrations to ensure that the true meaning of essential words is grasped. In Piagetian terms, the development of ideas and the language needed to think and talk about them makes the learner's mental 'model' richer and more accurate, and a better basis for further learning. This has the effect of making the learner 'more intelligent', in that he is now more able to learn from experience and to solve at least some future problems.

Application 14

For a community which you know well, identify at least five special features of its environment, including its attitude towards children, which you think might develop special abilities or disabilities in children and which are important points to consider when planning your teaching.

If possible work with fellow students and share ideas.

Further reading

The books listed for Chapter Seven are also relevant for this one, looking particularly at Wagner and Stevenson (ibid), p. 77, p. 166, p. 181 and p. 208 and Berry and Dasen (ibid), p. 141, p. 330 and p. 367.

CHAPTER NINE

The school's role in developing healthy personalities

As has already been mentioned, the school is not merely expected to be concerned with making sure that its pupils learn the content of the curriculum and syllabuses. It is also expected to contribute towards their development as healthy balanced people, able to fit in to their communities, to control their less acceptable impulses and to become what is known as 'socialised'. It is important, therefore, that teachers have some knowledge of how children's personal traits and qualities develop and how the schools can help. But there are other reasons why teachers need to know about personality development. For example, it is now realised that mental factors are only one part of successful learning, their personal qualities also being very important influences for all learners. Then too, there are some children whose personalities and abilities to adjust are so poorly developed that they could become serious problems unless understanding help is given at the right time. Finally, it is increasingly realised that the personality traits of teachers themselves, especially those which influence their attitudes towards their pupils, their work and their colleagues, are important factors in the education process.

As was the case when discussing intellectual development, we must make clear the words which have a different meaning when they are used in psychology from when they are used in everyday language. *Personality* is a word used to refer to the more or less permanent and consistent collection of attributes that go to make up an individual. These attributes include physical ones as well as those emotional and intellectual ones which make his behaviour and reactions fairly consistent while being different from everyone else's. The personality is made largely by the interaction of *temperament* and *experience* which makes *character*. *Temperament* is used to indicate an inherited tendency to develop certain personality traits, in much the same way as Intelligence 'A' represents an inherited potential for development, which is largely dependent on environmental circumstances for the course it actually takes. There is evidence that the existence and interaction of certain chemicals produced in the body, the *hormones*, can influence some temperamental traits. For example, an individual with an overactive thyroid gland is usually a highly energetic or even restless individual who will react to his environment in a different way from someone with a relatively under active thyroid, who is likely to react slowly and show considerable patience and lack of excitability. There seems also to be inborn differences in the excitability of nervous systems, some needing more outside stimulation than others before being aroused into sending impulses to the central nervous sytem and brain, and reacting to them. Such physical events are likely to produce certain personality traits which are typical of that individual. The third technical term, *character*, refers to the ways in which the interaction between temperament and environment shows itself in the individual's behaviour and reactions. Character can be likened to Intelligence 'B', and is largely what is identified and judged by others. The influence of parents, families, the community and the school combine to mould it into acceptable forms.

You will probably have noticed that the foregoing definitions offer a picture of personality development not very different from that of intellectual ability, in that it is the result of the interaction between inborn tendencies and environmental influences. Such a concept, while not being accepted by everyone, has proved to be of practical value to those involved in the upbringing and socialisation of children both inside and outside the school system. How the interaction happens is not known, though it is known that certain environments, cultural expectations and personal experiences are more likely than others to produce people with particular personality traits. For example, in cultures in which aggression and competitiveness are thought to be important masculine qualities, boys, even from early childhood, will be encouraged to play aggressively and competitively and later they will be rewarded by family and community approval for successfully showing such traits. By no means all the boys from such a community will be equally aggressive and competitive but, when compared with children brought up to value a different set of behaviours towards others, the proportion of aggressive people will be greater.

Most cultures and communities, though by no means all, require and expect different personality traits from their boys and girls and they bring them up accordingly. The temperamentally aggressive girls will probably learn to control their aggression or channel it into other more acceptable ways of behaving, such as being exceptionally persistent in their own opinions, or by dominating other girls; not all will be successful in their control, their actual behaviour being decided by the opportunities open to them and the reaction of others to aggressive behaviour. In the same way, the temperamentally non-aggressive boy may have to adjust to a low level of esteem among his fellows, which could lead to a lowering of his self confidence and possibly to underachievement. The more closed and unchanging the culture or community the narrower the range of personality traits likely to be tolerated and encouraged.

In Third World and multi-cultural countries, members of the population who move and settle into a newer, more culturally-mixed community may find that traits strongly developed in their early childhood are no longer appropriate. Their children, brought up in the newer situation, may find a clash between what their traditional home requires and what the wider community and school value and encourage.

It is very likely, too, that the teachings of the religion in which one is raised, especially those related to how one should live and behave, will influence important personality traits. For example, the Islamic emphasis on an active concern for the underprivileged which sees possessions both as something to be enjoyed by the owner as well as to be shared with others may modify personality traits and attitudes. The status of women vis-a-vis men must also have its effect. Those who are brought up as active Christians (perhaps in contrast to some who label themselves as Christians because they can think of no other label to use) may well place emphasis both on humility and love, and concern for others. Religions which accept the existence of the spirits of the dead, and sometimes the living, as having the power to influence their lives, for both good and evil, may well take less personal responsibility for themselves because of a feeling of relative powerlessness. The influence of religious beliefs on behaviour and personality is one which a teacher should consider, in the particular context in which he finds himself and his pupils.

The weight of evidence is, then, that, within inborn limits it is possible to encourage the development of favourable personality traits and discourage the development of unfavourable ones, though it is not possible to be certain how any one individual will react to a given situation. Nevertheless it is important for teachers to realise that they can have some influence on this important aspect of human development.

Personality development, then, involves a considerable amount of learning, most of it unconscious, i.e. the individual does not realise that he is learning to be a certain sort of person; it happens while he is doing and learning other things. From his earliest years, a child learns that some ways of behaving are acceptable and others are not. Certain personal traits are encouraged but he must learn to control and alter others if he is to achieve his purposes and be reasonably comfortable in, and adjusted to, his environment. An essential aspect of learning in personality development is that of self-control, or of finding ways of giving expression to temperamental traits which are accepted rather than rejected by others. This is usually a process of trial and error. A consistent and stable environment which helps a child to see clearly what are and are not acceptable ways of behaving, is likely to encourage balanced and stable personality traits. An inconsistent and confusing environment with no clear 'message' about how to interact with it may lead to a confused and uncontrolled individual, such traits possibly lasting over the years. As you can see, personality development and what is known as *discipline* are closely related, both being concerned with making an individual who is acceptable both to himself and others.

One of the ways in which it is thought that learning and personality interact is through the construction by each one of us of what is known as the *self-concept*. This refers to the mental picture or 'model' that one has of oneself. It is thought that, just as for Piaget, each individual builds up and continually modifies a personal mental model of the world as he experiences it, and acts as though the model is the same as the real world, so does every individual build up a mental model of himself. This self-concept includes not only his physical appearance and capabilities but also his mental abilities, his worth in the eyes of others, his relationships with family, friends and teachers, his ambitions and his fears. It acts as a sort of standard by which he will behave and make decisions, choices and so on. It is formed from the attitudes towards him and expectations of him that his family, friends, neighbours and teachers show and from the successes and failures which he has in all aspects of his life. When the attitudes and expections that come to him are consistent, the self-concept is simpler and more stable than if they are very variable. Perhaps one parent makes him feel that he is the most important person in the world whereas the other may be less sympathetic. A teacher who, by his willingness to encourage him, understand his mistakes and help him to achieve success, will add something important to the self-concept which will give him confidence to persist in school, even if he is not among the most able children. On the other hand, a teacher who praises and encourages only the already successful learners, giving the less successful ones the message that they are not worth bothering with, could cause long term distress or even harm.

As children get older, and especially into adolescence, they receive important 'messages' about themselves from their peers and companions. In many adolescent groups there is a sort of group self-concept which often determines how they will collectively behave as well as how individual members will behave within the group. Groups and gangs are important parts of an adolescent's social life and should not be discouraged, even though they may seem at times to be anti-social. Adolescent groups are usually made up of young people with some common experience and interest, so that the group's self-concept usually has a common source, each member finding something in it which matches and allows expression for his own personality traits. Sometimes the peer group is the only place where an individual is made to feel that he is of some worth and thus fills an important need for him. On a wider and more generalized scale, many school communities have a special sense of values which can affect the self-concept and consequently their pupils behaviour. For example, the author has studied the ethos, or sense of what is important, in the upper forms of a boys' secondary school, in which the school's general overemphasis on sporting ability which was shown by the praise given to the members of school teams and by the practice of selecting prefects and head boys from among them, led to a concept that hard academic study was unmanly. Many otherwise able boys seemed to underachieve academically deliberately, and those who were not at least competent and keen sportsmen often were unhappy among their fellows. The school, under a change of senior staff, rebuilt the ethos, or spirit, to include academic effort, whether or not it led to high achievement, and care was taken not to swing too far the other way. The result was a substantial improvement in academic standards and attitudes at all levels, with no real loss in sporting achievement.

Another example of a general ethos having an effect on individual and group self-concepts is of a co-educational secondary school in an already male-dominated society. Although there were women staff members, they were in a minority, all the posts of responsibility being held by men. The curriculum for boys and girls often differed. The offering of domestic science subjects to girls and technical ones to boys was probably not too harmful, but science subjects were offered only to 'A' streams, into which the most able boys were selected and no girls were even given the opportunity. They were relegated to the 'B' forms with the less-able boys. Even then, probably unconsciously, many teachers were seen to focus their teaching on the boys and either to ignore the girls or, at times, to laugh at their efforts. It is not surprising that very few girls achieved anything academically worthwhile, some being deeply reinforced in their belief that they were actually born less able than boys, while others tended to give up in despair when they could see that their efforts, even when as good as or better than those of the boys, were rejected. Such an ethos also tended to strengthen the belief by boys that girls and women are inferior to themselves and to men, which prevented them from gaining all that they could from the efforts of women staff in the school.

It is important for both school policy makers and curriculum planners, and for the teachers themselves, to remember that individuals tend to behave as though their self-concepts reflect the truth about themselves, especially when similar information comes in from several different sources. The teacher's own attitudes towards them and expectations from them often add to or alter aspects of the existing self-concept, especially when it strengthens or weakens their confidence in themselves. It is not helpful for an individual to be allowed to develop too high or too low an idea of his ability. It is important, therefore, that he be helped to build a realistic idea of his abilities and disabilities while at the same time seeing himself as someone of no less importance or worth because of his limitations. If he knows that he will receive understanding in his mistakes and help in correcting them he will see himself as someone who is at least persistent and a person worthy of a responsible adult's attention and respect. As a result, he is more likely to act in accordance with this picture of himself and so achieve more than he would otherwise do, while developing important qualities of personality.

Another way of viewing personality development which in no way goes against what has been said so far in this chapter, is in terms of what is sometimes called *need-achievement*. For example, Maslow has suggested that human beings have a number of inborn basic needs which must be satisfied if healthy and effective personalities are to be established. His proposed needs are built up in a sort of order of importance, the most basic having to be attained before the next level can be fully satisfied. The personality develops to the extent that the needs are or are not satisfied. The first four needs he calls *deficiency needs*, by which he means that if they are not properly fulfilled (or are *deficient*) the final personality may not develop completely or satisfactorily. The most basic need of all is rather obvious, i.e. the need for those things which enable the body to survive . . . food, oxygen, sleep, constant body temperature and so on. Next comes another survival need, a physically and psychologically secure environment and protection from dangers.

The third need is equally important for healthy personality growth but perhaps is less consciously appreciated, and that is the need for a feeling of being loved, of belonging in an emotionally warm group. Deprivation here is more widespread than in the other two areas mentioned, but fortunately it is still relatively rare. What is perhaps missing is enough evidence to convince the individual that he is really loved and accepted. Research has shown that an inadequate fulfilment of this need can lead to problems in later emotional adjustment and may certainly be a handicap to school learning. The fourth deficiency need is related to the self-concept that we discussed earlier and includes the need for self esteem, to feel good about oneself, to have some skills and successes (sometimes known as *mastery*) and to be respected by other people as someone worthwhile. The way in which this fourth need is fulfilled may vary, or, rather, the successes and mastery which satisfy it may vary, but the need itself is a strong one and very important for healthy personal development and adjustment to life.

Maslow's final need is what he calls *self-actualisation* or *self-fulfilment*. This is a *growth need* rather than a deficiency one, and includes the ways in which an individual can develop the potential that he has, and it suggests that there must be a well-graded and planned opportunity for him to acquire the needed knowledge and skills and to develop his intellectual abilities. It also suggests the need for opportunities for him eventually to become an independent individual, able to accept

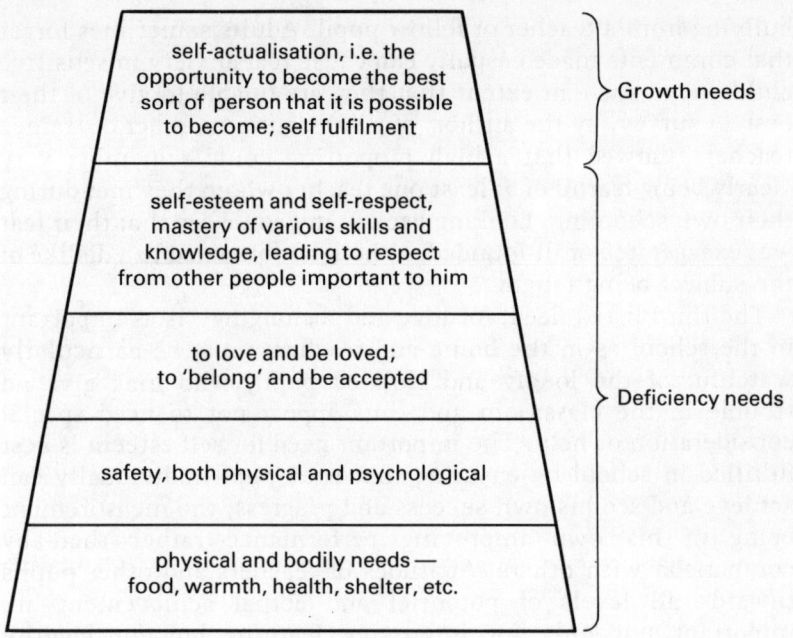

responsibility for himself and others while being a well-adjusted member of his world. The diagram above summarises the 'hierarchy' of human needs as described by Maslow, the most fundamental ones being at the bottom. Although the human needs are arranged in order, earlier ones having to be fulfilled before later ones can be dealt with, one must not forget that every individual must have all of them fulfilled all through his life, the parent and teacher as much as the child.

Not everyone accepts Maslow's theory or any other theory of personality in its entirety. However, it provides useful reminders that the school organization and especially the class teacher must ensure that each need is fulfilled for each pupil to the best of their ability. Some aspects of the first need, nutrition and physical health, were discussed earlier in the book, the point being made that it may be necessary for schools to take some action in exceptional cases. The second need, to feel and to be physically safe before effective learning and development can take place, is also obvious. Less obvious is the need for psychological security, freedom from the fear and excessive anxiety which sometimes exists among children whose homes are unsatisfactory or who have experienced unduly harsh and insensitive treatment and bullying from a teacher or fellow pupil. Adults sometimes forget that comments made casually can cause real anxiety in sensitive children, to such an extent that they are unable to give of their best. A survey, by the author, of a substantial number of trainee teachers showed that a high proportion could remember very clearly being fearful of at least one teacher whom they met during their own schooling. Looking back many could see that their fear was exaggerated or ill-founded, although it often led to a dislike of the subject being taught.

The third listed need, for love and 'belonging', is as important in the school as in the home and teachers must be particularly watchful of the lonely and isolated pupil, who may give no trouble in the classroom and thus appear not to need special consideration or help. The important need for self esteem is best fulfilled in school by ensuring that each pupil individually can achieve and see his own success and progress, the measurement being of his own improving performance rather than by comparison with others. Attitudes of teachers and other pupils towards all levels of potential and actual achievement are important not only for improving learning but for healthy personality development and adjustment.

Self-actualisation comes from the fulfilment of all the other needs, with the possibility of increasing independence and decision making in a situation where firm, warm support exists to give confidence. A contribution to this is made in a school where the rules of discipline are not so fixed and uniform that there is no room for individuals to accept personal responsibility for themselves and others. Adequate fulfilment of the basic psychological needs, especially when it is done in both home and school, should lead to the development of healthy balanced personalities, no two individuals being exactly alike but all being sufficiently confident and flexible to adapt to circumstances and achieve whatever promise their abilities allow.

Now that the circumstances in which favourable personality development is thought to take place have been discussed, it is necessary to recognize that a teacher, or a whole school, can achieve only a certain amount. In every school there are individuals with major traits which can influence their subsequent progress in personal development. It is important not to attach too firm a personality-type label to an individual, because of the danger of it becoming a self-fulfilling prophecy, i.e. something that happens because you expect it to happen. Nevertheless it is important for individual weaknesses to be recognized by the teacher and suitable steps taken where possible. For instance, some individuals consistently react suddenly and impulsively, without giving themselves time to think through exactly what is to be done and how to do it. Consequently, they may make unnecessary mistakes and waste quite a lot of their own time. Often such an individual is highly intelligent, his progress being hampered by personality traits and learning habits. A teacher can help by gently making the individual conscious of this characteristic and setting him a challenge to overcome it, in a positive rather than a negative and hurtful way.

Another fairly common trait is lack of persistence and a tendency to stop making an effort when a difficulty is encountered. This may be the result of one of several possibilities. Perhaps at home he has not been expected to make an effort, or perhaps his efforts in the past have met with scorn and rejection so that he withdraws in self-protection. A teacher, with understanding and careful encouragement and grading of work, can help a pupil to overcome this trait, restoring confidence when it is lacking and reducing feelings of insecurity and anxiety where they exist.

A potentially harmful characteristic can show in the excessively persistent and hard-working individual who sets himself far too high a standard of achievement and has to put too much effort into keeping it up. It may not seem a cause for concern to the teacher, especially when such excessive persistence is crowned with academic success, but it is important that such individuals develop a sense of balance in their lives to counteract the later possibility of crippling disappointment and anxiety when sheer hard work does not prevent failure; more flexibility of character is needed.

A final example of the problem individual which is often met is one who consistently seems to be against authority, and adopts a generally aggressive and negative attitude towards the requirements of the school. This trait is more commonly found in older children and can show itself by persistent refusal to obey any school rules despite frequent punishment or it may lead to truancy. Such an individual causes considerable trouble in a school, especially once the characteristic has become deeply established. It is also one of the more difficult ones to handle, if only because there can be several possible causes. The most frequent one can be identified in terms of Maslow's psychological needs, especially the need for success, the esteem of others and acceptance. The punishment which is so regularly meted out for his negative behaviour is sometimes the only sign of recognition from the school that the child exists as an individual, and his wrong-doing may be an attempt to fill his unconsciously felt shortcomings, if only by making him a hero in the eyes of some of his school fellows.

As can be seen, there is no clear cut recipe for dealing with personality problems and the behaviour resulting from them. All a teacher can reasonably do is to get to know all his pupils, be aware of possible adverse personality traits and try to ensure that he does everything that he can to make his classroom a place where both group and individual needs are fulfilled. Special attention to the few pupils with potential problems will complete the picture.

The teacher's personality

It has sometimes been said that teachers should be selected for training and appointed to posts, not only for their academic competence, but also for their personality traits, since their interaction with their pupils is an important factor in successful teaching. Unfortunately, despite the existence of a number of tests which seem to identify some major personality traits, not much progress has been made in identifying those people who will make good teachers, largely because the ideal characteristics for a teacher are not fully known. As a result, there is almost as much variety among the personalities of teachers as there is among their pupils. In countries where there is a wide range of career openings, other than teaching, for intelligent young men and women there is usually some sensible self-selection into the teaching profession, especially when its status and salary structure are not inferior to the alternatives. Unfortunately other considerations usually prevail so that not everyone entering the teaching profession is naturally well suited to it. A major responsibility for teacher-education programmes, therefore, is to develop personality traits and their attendant attitudes and actions which have proved in practice to be the most suitable. It is unlikely that such programmes have much effect on the basic or *core* personality but they can encourage students to look carefully and realistically at themselves so that they become aware of areas where they need to make a conscious effort to behave towards their pupils and their work in suitable ways. A book such as this tries to give the student a clear picture of the needs of the learner and the things that education should try to achieve. A teacher who genuinely tries to fulfill these cannot help showing good personal qualities. But more than this is needed and every teacher should, at intervals, look realistically at himself, how he behaves in the classroom and his attitudes towards the individual pupils in it, at his attitudes towards his colleagues and to the profession of teaching and at his motives for the actions that he takes. If he can see himself as his pupils see him and likes what he sees, he is well on the way towards becoming the sort of person that they need him to be.

The teacher, too, has a self-concept which has built up over the years and, as with all adults, this is many-sided. Although there is a general tendency to act in certain ways, different qualities and characteristics are shown in different situations and to different people. The particular aspects that a teacher needs to become aware of and to modify where necessary are those of 'teacher' and 'colleague'. Once he knows the personal qualities most likely to lead to successful teaching he should be able to construct a 'mental model' of such a person and then compare his perception of himself with the ideal. Possibly the most important trait for a teacher to possess is the maturity and honesty to look at himself and his behaviour, to see how far they match up to the needs of his profession. One such need is the ability to put the requirements of others, especially those of his pupils, before those of himself. We have all met teachers who use the power and authority which their work gives them to satisfy some gap in their own self-esteem, and this has a noticeable effect on their pupils and colleagues. Certainly a mature teacher can and should find personal satisfaction in his work, but this should be because of his achievements in educating his pupils in the fullest sense. Good relationships with his colleagues, the ability to communicate freely with them and with his pupils' parents and, above all, a commitment to the total job, are also the qualities of a mature and successful teacher. It is indeed possible for a teacher to develop personal qualities which may eventually become a complete part of himself, having the added benefit of making him a happier and more acceptable individual in other spheres of his life.

The implications for teachers of what has been discussed in this chapter are much the same in whatever system and at whatever level they teach. The range of individual characteristics among their pupils will always be wide, while their psychological needs which must be satisfied will be much the same. This means that all teachers should become as familiar as possible with the characteristics which their pupils' homes and cultural backgrounds are likely to have encouraged, especially those which may affect those attitudes and motives which influence their adjustment to, and achievement in, school. If the teacher himself is from a culture or social class which values behaviour and characteristics which are different from those of most of his pupils, he will need to be very sensitive to the possible gap between himself and his pupils. This sensitivity must extend towards colleagues and, just as important, towards his pupils' parents, who also have their psychological needs, if full co-operation in educating their children is to be obtained.

As has been said before, certain cultures and sub-cultures tend to emphasize the need for particular personal qualities which are likely to have an effect on educational progress and needs. Social psychologists studying, for example, groups whose traditional culture has remained unchanged for many generations and who resist change, have found that many of their members have an exaggerated tendency to accept without question the opinions of their elders, or of the majority, even when the evidence does not support them. It is easy to see how individuals possessing this characteristic could be at a disadvantage in a school which values independence of thought. They may be at a further disadvantage when they return to their traditional homes after their schooling has encouraged individuality and intellectual self-confidence.

In contrast, some sub-cultures allow their children so much freedom of action, especially when among adults, that teachers find it difficult to harness and discipline their learning so as to enable them to reap the full benefits of their schooling. It would be impossible in a book such as this to discuss all the likely culturally-encouraged personality variables. All we can do here is to create awareness among teachers of some of the possibilities in the hope that they will make it their business to become knowledgeable about their pupils and the cultural norms of their homes so that they can have a greater understanding of their educational needs and how best to help them to continue to grow towards healthy, mature adulthood.

Application 15, Part 1

1 In a class of children whom you know well:
a) List the names of those who appear to have most of the following

characteristics, which are indicators of a *positive self-concept*:
1) welcomes new situations and experiences,
2) seems to be a happy individual,
3) makes friends easily with other children,
4) rarely seems to need to help of a teacher but seeks it when necessary,
5) trusts his teachers and other adults, even when he does not know them very well,
6) talks freely and is eager to share his interests and ideas, though he may not be a good listener,
7) has ideas of his own which may differ from those of the group; is imaginative,
8) is co-operative and usually obeys reasonable rules,
9) can usually control his own behaviour.

b) List the names of those who appear to have characteristics which are mainly the opposite of those listed above (i.e. a *negative self-concept*):

2 In the case of the negative self-concept what could you, as a teacher, do to help? When you have recorded your ideas look at the suggestions given in Part 2 and compare them with your own ideas.

3 How do *you* rate on the listed characteristics? Is your self concept a positive or a negative one? Discuss your view of yourself with a fellow student who knows you well. If you have negative traits, try consciously to act more in accordance with the positive ones. You will eventually find that you are, in fact, becoming more positive, which is important not only for your own development as a person but also for your pupils, who need their teacher to be someone in whom they can have confidence. If you have no confidence in yourself you cannot easily make your pupils confident in you.

Application 15, Part 2

Here are some suggestions for helping a pupil to develop a more positive self-concept.
1 Make sure that what you plan for him to learn is within his capacity but challenging enough for him to feel that he has achieved something worthwhile.
2 Make sure that he feels that you care about *him* by giving him verbal encouragement, listening to him attentively.
3 Accept the things that he does, but always be honest in your comments to him, while praising some aspects of his behaviour and work even when he is not completely successful. Take the trouble to help him with his mistakes.
4 Ask for his ideas and suggestions and make him feel as though they are important to you and the class.
5 Show him that you respect him and value him as a human being, irrespective of his ability and progress.

6 Be patient with him.
7 Give him chances within his ability to make decisions and choices, though being sure that they will not overwhelm him.

Further reading

Reading further articles in Wagner and Stevenson, Berry and Dasen, etc., would give you insight into some of the influences, especially cultural ones, on the development of personalities. It is important to remember that there is a close and essential link between personality traits which must be developed and what the society needs in its members. No one text can prescribe the details. Enquire in the Social Anthropology Departments (or Departments of Social Sciences) in local colleges and universities for any books and research papers which may have been produced locally.

CHAPTER TEN

Discipline and the school's resonsibility for moral development

An almost universal anxiety which students and teachers have at the beginning of their careers is that they may not be able to maintain discipline in their classes. They have visions of losing control to the extent that their pupils will at best ignore them and at worst become noisily riotous. They would all like their training courses to give them a simple set of rules which will guarantee that their pupils will remain obedient and orderly. Unfortunately, no such set of rules exists (or, at least, rules that will not seriously hamper the learning processes), although there are some general principles which, if carefully interpreted, can be of great help in making sure that both learners and teachers can do their work properly. As an introduction to these we need to look at important aspects of discipline, both in the light of our psychological knowledge and of the overall task of the school and its teaching staff.

The term *discipline*, as it applies to the school, can be looked at in two main ways. Firstly, it is a necessity if the school is to do its job so that individuals and groups can reap the full benefit from it. Secondly, it is a contributor to the personal development of the pupils themselves. In the first case, it suggests that there is in the school an established and expected pattern of behaviour which all pupils are required to accept, both for their own good and that of the group, class or school as a whole. It is thus a social concept. All social groups, whether they be an extended family, a small nuclear family, the neighbourhood, a church, a club or a youth gang, have their own rules which ensure that they survive and fulfill their purpose. As we have seen, one of the universal psychological needs is to belong to, and feel part of, a group. This means that there is a strong inborn tendency for individuals to obey the rules of behaviour so that they can become acceptable members of the group. If it is any comfort to would-be teachers, most children *want* to feel that they are part of their class and school and will generally obey quite a lot of imposed rules of behaviour even when these limit their immediate personal desires. On the other hand, we have all experienced occasions when individuals, or, even worse, groups, either ignore or defy some rules, becoming what are thought of as discipline problems. There are many possible reasons for this, some of the more serious perhaps stemming from abnormal development patterns which a few individuals have. Most disciplinary problems, however, arise from such things as not knowing what behaviour is required because the rules are unclear or contradictory. Then, too, the rules may be so widely different from the individual's normal needs that he is willing to risk disapproval to satisfy them. Unreasonable rules with no clear social purpose may also be rejected and hence themselves cause disciplinary problems, while a teacher who is blatantly unjust in his attitudes and actions towards his pupils may find difficulty in controlling his pupils.

Discipline in this sense, then, is a socialisation process in which the pupils are taught to conform to certain types of behaviour, to reject others and to accept the school's decision as to what things and actions are or are not important. This means that they are taught a specific set of personal and group values. The actual rules and expected behaviours required by the school as a whole, and each teacher individually, are passed on partly by tradition, partly by direct statement by those in authority and partly through a gradual process of learning by example or by trial and error. Acceptable behaviour is 'rewarded' and unacceptable behaviour is 'punished', about which more will be said later. The second, and more important aim of the disciplinary and socialisation processes used in the home, the school and the wider society , is to produce adults who can be responsible for their own decisions about how to behave in all aspects of their lives and can contribute sensibly to the community decisions which are an important part of many African societies.

It includes their attitudes towards the behaviour acceptable to their culture, as well as their willingness to keep the law of the established authority and to fulfill the obligations which being a member of a group implies. It also includes the development of such traits as truthfulness, respect for other people's rights as human beings, attitudes towards their own and other peoples's property, acceptance of the customary family responsibilities and sexual behaviours and attitudes. Discipline in this sense is seen as contributing to the development of those moral standards and values that are needed by the wider society in which the individual lives.

Classroom discipline

Let us first of all go into more detail about that aspect of school discipline, sometimes called classroom management, which is concerned with ensuring that the best conditions are established and maintained for learning to take place. It is sometimes thought that such discipline can be imposed by the teacher solely by wielding some sort of power over the pupils. This is possible to some extent but unless it also takes into account the psychological needs and developmental levels of the pupils, the maintenance of control is likely to become increasingly difficult for the teacher, who usually finds himself having to adopt ever harsher threats and actual punishments to keep a semblance of order. Under such conditions, the intended learning is likely to be reduced, the individuals who are most affected often being those least likely to need drastic discipline, i.e. the most timid.

Another less successful technique which is sometimes used for keeping control of a class is based on the principle that 'Satan finds work for idle hands to do, so keep them busy all the time'. Indeed, children do need to be kept actively involved in learning but all too often teachers give a great deal of unnecessary written work just to keep the class occupied, which adds very little to the education process. Such work is sometimes called 'busy' work and consists of long repetitive exercises which demand very little thought. One is sometimes surprised how much 'busy' work some children, especially younger ones, are prepared to do without protest, possibly because they feel that they are, at least, unlikely to make mistakes, which in itself is something of an achievement. Other teachers may worry about allowing noise to be made in their classrooms and plan work which keeps their pupils in their own seats and not sharing ideas and activities with other members of the class. Their teaching scope is limited by lack of confidence, both in themselves and in their pupils.

A well-managed classroom must start with thorough advance

planning by the teacher, along the lines suggested in Chapter Six when discussing how to enable effective learning to take place. It must, indeed, be a busy, active place in which the pupils and the teacher know that they are on the same side, working together to achieve something worthwhile. Such a classroom is likely to establish mutual respect and a mild reproof or expression of disappointment on the part of the teacher will be enough to bring the pupils back under control. The planning must include detail about how confusion and wasteful pauses are to be avoided when children move into their groups, set up an experiment or collect their materials. Inexperienced teachers, especially, can reduce their anxieties about class control by visualising exactly how each stage of the lesson will move into the next one, planning every action needed.

Another feature of good discipline often involves a reduction, rather than an increase, in the number of formal rules which exist. Of course, rules are necessary and all pupils must become aware of them and encouraged to obey them. Many such rules are designed to make the classroom and school places where most people are comfortable; they are social in their origin and intent. Cleanliness and tidiness of surroundings, not being excessively noisy or disruptive when others are working, taking care of communal property etc., come into this category, as do punctuality and not rushing about to the danger of others. The normal courtesies expected by the general community should continue to be observed. The best way to establish such rules is by quiet persistence and a good example by the teacher. But there may be traditional rules which have no real purpose and which can be counter-productive, such as not allowing children to leave their seats without permission, or to read a non-prescribed book when they have completed required tasks, or to discuss their work quietly with their neighbours. It is a healthy exercise for teachers to review their rules and expectations every now and then, to see if there is any area where more freedom of choice of behaviour can be given without losing the essential orderliness which children need and seek in their learning environments.

In essence, then, good classroom management is that which enables the sort of psychological needs proposed by Maslow and others to be satisfied. In almost all cases of poor discipline of an individual or group, there has been in the past, and probably still is, an unfilled basic need. Sometimes a teacher inherits a problem class or individual and he may have to adopt remedial measures, some of which will be discussed later. Most frequently, however, especially if the problem gets worse rather than better as time passes, he has overlooked an important need. Taking Maslow's hierarchy, he should look carefully at each level (see page 125), including the most basic physiological one of nutrition and ventilation. The most likely deficiency in the second category is that of psychological security. Children sometimes feel threatened by an inconsistent teacher whose temper is uncertain, so that they themselves tend to act unpredictably. The third category, of love and belonging, has already been discussed in the context of effective learning and personality development and probably is the key feature of good discipline and control. Children who feel that their teacher has a genuine affection and concern for them and ensures that they feel accepted by him and by other pupils, are unlikely to cause serious disciplinary problems. The 'messages' which the teacher gives to his pupils are conveyed through the attention that he gives them, the way in which he knows them individually and is prepared to help them, the loyalty and respect that he shows them, and his ability to criticize them constructively when they do not live up to their standards. Similarly, the fourth Maslow stage, of self-esteem, which grows from the fulfillment of the previous one, is essential to sound discipline. Problem children are often those who have not been able to establish a feeling of self-respect because others, including their teachers, have not convinced them that they are worthy of respect.

Good group and individual discipline, then, is not something that must be established *before* learning can take place. It is largely established *through* their learning and their total classroom experience. The point can be illustrated by an example from a large boys' high school, in which the lowest ability streams were proving difficult to control and were obviously achieving very little real learning. Most teachers disliked teaching these forms and some showed it unconsciously, by poor preparation and little attempt to interest the boys. Punishments abounded. Groups of student teachers, with the full co-operation and approval of the Headmaster, planned special programmes in several school subjects, introducing a variety of different and practical learning methods such as films, outside visits, model making, demonstrations to other forms and so on. Much of their basic work was individualised so that each boy could see his own progress, and special efforts were made to meet their parents to discuss their sons' progress in a constructive and realistically optimistic way. The result was that not only did the attainment of the boys, almost without exception, improve greatly but their attitudes to classwork, homework, and the school itself improved. Their confidence and general self control and class discipline were also noticeably improved, as was their school attendance. Which of the remedial measures taken had the most impact cannot be identified. It is likely that they all, in combination, fulfilled Maslow's psychological needs more satisfactorily than had hitherto been the case. It is worth noting that, at first, many members of the school staff, while glad to be relieved of some teaching, were sceptical of the programme. Even at the end they were not willing to accept that it would have more than a short term effect, the most resistant being the least effective teachers with the greatest discipline problems.

Application 16

1   If possible, undertake this task with a fellow student, comparing your observations and analyses.
Arrange to spend at least four timetabled periods with the same class in a school catering for the age range of pupils which you eventually hope to teach. Note the ways in which their teacher or teachers handle any disciplinary problems which occur, as well as the most common types of misbehaviour. Did these differ with different teachers or in different subjects?
The following questions should help you:
1   What were the most frequent misbehaviours?
2   How many children were involved in them and how many times?
3   What did the teacher do about them?
4   How successful were their efforts?
5   Did the disciplinary actions disrupt the whole class or focus closely on the culprits?
6   What do you think were the main causes of the problems encountered?
    e.g. uncertainty about what they were expected to do?
    boredom?
    friendly high spirits?
    lack of respect for the teacher?
    fatigue?
    trying to be noticed, by the teacher or fellow pupils?
    poor class organization?
    insufficient chance to achieve something worthwhile, etc.?
7   Did the class teacher apparently ignore any incident of indiscipline? If so, with what effect?
8   Were there any individuals who were persistent offenders? In what ways?

9   Was the general atmosphere in the class
    happy and relaxed?
    co-operative?
    noisy?
    quarrelsome?
    reluctant?
    indifferent, etc?

If possible discuss your observations with the class teacher whom you watched, making it clear that you are not presuming to criticize.

   2   Look back at your own most recent teaching experience, or arrange to have some experience. What discipline and class management problems did you encounter? What did you do about them? What do you think were their origins?
   e.g. lack of detailed planning?
   children not knowing exactly what they were to do?
   too much or too little work?
   too little direct involvement in the learning?
   children's interest not captured? if so why?
   your own inexperience and lack of confidence leading the pupils to test how you react?
   your expectations or those of the school were too different from the traditional discipline of their home? if so, how did they differ?

So far very little has been said directly about the place of rewards and punishments in developing and maintaining discipline, though their rôle in motivation for learning was mentioned in an earlier chapter. Some people tend to think of these two aspects of education as including only tangible and direct items, like the receiving of something pleasurable such as prizes, high marks, direct praise and privileges or, conversely, low marks, scoldings, withholding of pleasurable activities or even physical assault. These are, of course, rewards and punishments but, to the extent that they are used at all, they are usually reserved for the extreme cases, the high achievers, the seriously ill-disciplined, the defiant and so on. In a classroom in which real efforts are made to fulfill the pupil's psychological needs, the need-satisfaction is usually enough reward. Disappointment and disapproval expressed by a respected and concerned teacher is often enough of a punishment.

In recent years attempts have been made to deal with some persistent offenders through a technique known as *behaviour modification*. It involves the teacher, first of all, in closely analysing what the unsuitable behaviour is and what sort of behaviour should be aimed at instead. Often the culprit himself is consulted quietly and privately by the teacher. Others have, with the culprit's approval, enlisted the help of the rest of the class. The main principle of behaviour modification is that the teacher shows quiet approval whenever the culprit is showing the desired behaviour, especially at times when he would have previously shown the undesired behaviour. As far as possible he ignores instances of bad behaviour, especially when it is unlikely to harm others. In this way, a positive attempt is made to reinforce (i.e. to reward by approval) good behaviour rather than bad, which is often the result of a feeling of lack of recognition and attention. It is most likely that the very fact of the teacher showing his concern to the individual and trying to help him is the main source of any cure. The process of behaviour modification has been used fairly successfully by at least one group of high school pupils, who decided that they would try it on a teacher who was notorious for his acid tongue, impatience and inconsistency. They made a point of showing a high degree of interest and pleasure when their teacher was pleasant and patient, and quietly ignored him or remained impassive when he showed his less pleasant and more destructive sides. Although the teacher was unaware of how his behaviour was being modified, he gradually began to show more of the positive than the negative traits. He even boasted to his colleagues that he now had this class, which had previously been difficult, 'eating out of his hand'.

Even though very few teachers consciously use behaviour modification techniques to attain discipline, a great many use it, without realising, to reinforce misbehaviour. Such teachers use a great deal of verbal disapproval in their classes, constantly telling the class or individuals to sit down, stop talking, get on with their work, not to call out the answers and so on. There is nothing wrong with these instructions as such, and they are sometimes necessary, but research shows that in classrooms where there is a constant stream of instructions the misbehaviour is being encouraged instead of reduced. A teacher who finds himself constantly having to repeat such reminders should look more closely to see whether what he thinks he is trying to prevent is *really* misbehaviour and thus not to be tolerated, and, if it is, the circumstances in which it most often occurs. Some adjustment in class management techniques could improve matters.

The use of more drastic punishment, such as serious deprivation of liberty or of much-enjoyed activities, isolation of the individual, parading the culprit and his sins before the whole school or, where it is still permitted, corporal punishment, is very rarely a long-term cure and is more likely to do harm than good. Individuals who do not respond to normal and relatively quick disapprovals and sanctions probably need special and skilled investigation into all their circumstances. One can understand the frustration of a busy teacher or headmaster when confronted with an apparently incorrigible individual. He may feel that real punishment is called for, but there is a danger of the punishment being given to relieve the feelings of the staff rather than to help the culprit. All too often, it is further proof to the culprit that everyone is against him, which in turn is likely to lead him into more trouble as he uses anti-social ways to adjust to what, to him, is an unfair situation.

It is time now to move the focus of this discussion from the discipline thought necessary to enable the school and its members to do their jobs, to the development of longer-term moral values in the individual pupils. By *moral* development is meant the building up of a consistent set of values and ideas which can become a basis for making personal decisions about how to behave in relation to to other people and the society in which we find ourselves. It consists eventually of a set of principles which, at best, enables us to react properly in new situations where rules which we may have previously accepted do not apply. As you can see, the concept of morality is much more than obedience and acceptance; it is a process of making one's own decisions. The details of desired attitudes and behaviour vary from culture to culture, group to group and even from generation to generation. The processes whereby they are developed, however, are now thought to be universal, much as the processes whereby intellectual skills develop are universal, details and emphases varying according to the demands made on the individual by the environment.

Most of us gradually absorb the accepted principles and values from our immediate and extended families, the neighbourhood, the school, religious instruction, friendship groups, work, the mass media and so on. By the time we are adults we have built these principles and values into our self-concepts and try to behave in accordance with them. The truth is, however, that very few individuals behave with complete consistency, perhaps being scrupulously honest and truthful, or kind and patient in some situations and not in others. This inconsistency is much more frequent among people whose experience has been of several different and changing sets of moral values. Since the world for most people is becoming increasingly complex, the more so for those living in rapidly developing and multi-cultural countries, it is increasingly important that the school tries to establish, not a fixed set of values which will remain true for all time, but the capacity for individuals to weigh up alternative actions and attitudes and to select those that seem most likely to lead to the best result.

A major purpose of the great religions and their teachings is to develop in young people a knowledge and acceptance of their main moral laws and rules of behaviour. The widespread Koranic schools, which may be attended in addition to the more secular schools, place great emphasis on learning from the Koran. Schools with a Christian basis ensure that the major teachings of Christ as well as the Laws of Moses are learned. The social and culture group to which each person belongs has its own rules of 'morality' in the sense that we are using it here. It is not normally the job of the school to substitute one set of moral attitudes and beliefs for another. Rather, it is their job to help their pupils eventually to be able to make decisions about their behaviour within their own social setting. In order to do this, they need some knowledge about how what one could call 'moral thinking' develops and matures, so that they can encourage the process.

Briefly, Kohlberg says that moral growth proceeds in a succession of stages, each one based on, and gradually emerging from, the previous one. The stages are universal and hence a part of the inborn human potential and as such are not dependent on culture or sub-culture. Morality is thus not a collection of fixed traits, or something that we do or do not have, but a tendency to behave in a certain way which is to some extent related to the stage of development that has been reached. Although the stages are loosely linked to the chronological age, as are those of cognitive development, there is considerable variation from individual to individual. There is also variation in the consistency and efficiency with which individuals function at each stage, the variations being related to both genetic potential (probably intellectual) and to the opportunity which their various environments have afforded for development. It is this last aspect which is particularly important for the school and other socialising agencies.

Kohlberg identifies six stages of development, distributed over three levels and he describes the sorts of thinking which are typical for each stage. Stages 1 and 2 at Level One he calls *Pre-Conventional* and suggests that they are strongest in most children at least until six or seven years of age, and often longer. The behaviour of someone in Stage 1 is much influenced by the way that people in his life react to him. He is obedient in order to avoid punishment or uncomfortable reactions, and he accepts that much of his world and the people in it are more powerful than he is. He may even believe that 'might is right', i.e. that the most powerful have a right to things just because they are the strongest. Children at this stage of development need to receive clear and consistent reactions to their behaviour since most of their learning about how and how not to behave is the result of a process called *conditioning*, i.e. they learn how to behave next time from the reaction to their present behaviour, acceptable actions being met with pleasant results and the unacceptable ones being met with unpleasant results. The child obeys the rules to avoid punishment and has no personal idea of right and wrong beyond this. This stage gradually merges into Stage 2 of the Pre-Conventional level, in which he behaves largely to please himself. He may be prepared to take the needs of other into account but only while they also satisfy his own.

Level Two is called *Conventional*, it also being divided into two stages, i.e. Stages 3 and 4. In Stage 3 the child tends to adopt behaviour which he knows pleases others, giving him a sense of pleasure at 'being good'. He is now beginning to realize that his behaviour has a social basis. As this develops into Stage 4 he begins to accept that he must obey the rules of those in authority without question because it maintains the stability and safety of his own and the wider environment. Children at this age are very anxious that the rules of whatever games they play are clearly stated and strictly obeyed. Although this level mainly covers the pre-adolescent years, in fact very many adults function a good deal of the time at this level because it leads to a generally comfortable and undemanding existence. Most of them are not averse to breaking the rules when it is to their advantage and they are not likely to be found out and thus be made uncomfortable.

Level Three, the *Post-Conventional* is, says Kohlberg, unlikely to develop much before adolescence, though research suggests that, as with formal operational reasoning, some children, at least occasionally, function at this level earlier, while many do not appear to achieve it at all with any degree of consistency and efficiency. The first part, Stage 5, is characterised by the individual's belief that moral behaviour is the result of an agreement with other people to behave to the general good of the community. Laws given by the properly established authority are to be obeyed to the extent that they preserve human rights. It is as though the individual has consciously agreed on a contract with fellow human beings to do nothing to harm them. Indeed, he would hope to promote their good. At Stage 6, the highest level, moral behaviour is based on a universal, ethical principle, laws being obeyed only when they do not conflict with that principle, which is that all human beings have a right to equality and personal dignity. It is significant that the great and lasting religions and philosophies of the world teach this principle above all others, as in the Christian 'Golden Rule' of doing unto others what you would wish them to do to you. Other major religions achieve the same purpose by teaching that all human beings are part of God Himself. On the other hand, many great religions went through a period where a set of specific rules for behaviour were established, such as the Ten Commandments of Moses, unquestioning obedience to which was necessary at the time to preserve the unity and structure of the nomadic Israelite society.

The best way to illustrate and clarify Kohlberg's analysis is by looking at a series of typical replies to an imaginary problem which he put to numbers of people at different age levels. The problem was in the form of a story in which a woman was dying of a rare disease for which there was only one drug likely to save her. The drug was discovered by a chemist who was the only person who had a supply of it. Although it was quite expensive to make he asked the woman's husband, Heinz, to pay ten times what it cost him to make. Heinz tried unsuccessfully to borrow the money or to persuade the chemist to let him have it cheaper, or to allow him to pay for it later. So Heinz broke into the man's store and stole the drug, thus saving his wife's life. Kohlberg asked many people whether they thought Heinz was right in acting as he did, and to explain the reasons for their answers. The replies he received could be organized into his six stages, roughly, though not completely, in line with his age and ability progression.

At Stage 1, the answers were either that he should not have stolen the drug because he could go to jail, or that he was right to do it because it did not cost the chemist that much to make. Stage 2 answers said that he either should not have stolen it because by the time he got out of jail his wife would probably be dead anyway so it was a waste of time, or he should have done it because he needed his wife to look after him. At Level Two, Stage 3, those who disapproved did so because Heinz and his family and friends would be ashamed of his stealing, while those who approved said that it was good that he should look after his wife. Stage 4 at this level showed either approval because he would otherwise have been responsible for his wife's death, or disapproval because he broke the law of the land. As you can see, these reasons are all concrete and directly related to the best interests of Heinz himself or those around him.

At Level Three, Stage 5, answers moved into the realm of general principles, some saying that no law ought to allow anyone to lose their life to satisfy someone's greed, and others that he was wrong to steal because there might have been someone else even more in need of the drug than Heinz's wife. Finally, at Stage 6, the universal principle was clearly shown, that Heinz's conscience put human life above human greed but , having stolen the drug, he should then have given himself up to the police and taken his punishment, because his conscience would tell him that no society could allow individuals to take the law into their own hands. He could also, they said, set about using lawful means to have exploitation, such as that shown by the chemist, made illegal. An interesting side exercise would be to assess the level of moral functioning by the chemist, which seems to be very immature and at Level One, based on the idea that 'might is right', and 'my needs are more important than your needs'.

What, then, are the major educational implications for a stage-related concept of moral development such has been proposed by Kohlberg? If he is right in suggesting that, despite its universal order of progression, there are a number of external circumstances that encourage or delay development, then it is important that any school, whose programme includes in its aim the development of moral values, should consider seriously the extent to which its present organization contributes to development and how to improve it. School rules and ways of establishing and maintaining disciplined behaviour should be examined to see if they fit in with what can be expected of the age group concerned. At younger age levels a certain number of clearly defined, fixed rules are necessary and, as was said earlier, most children accept them most of the time because they make them feel safe and comfortable. But as adolescence approaches, while essential rules of behaviour must still exist, opportunities are needed for pupils to come to understand the value and purpose of each one and to make more suitable rules where necessary. There have been a number of successful experiments in allowing pupils, under adult supervision, to conduct some of their own disciplinary affairs, especially when they themselves have been made aware of the need for a standard of conduct and the results of breaking it. Young people who have had this sort of experience generally attain a higher level of personal behaviour because they have been helped to develop a sense of social responsibility. On the other hand, young people from very rigid and rule-bound schools where pupils are not encouraged to question or even think about the rules, may well be less mature in their personal behaviour.

Kohlberg suggested a number of programmes aimed at encouraging moral development, based on his finding that, while children rarely act with complete consistency at only one developmental level, they can be helped to think and act at a higher level in several ways. Once their present, most often used level is identified they can often be helped towards the next higher level by being encouraged to discuss among themselves and with their teachers some of the important moral issues of the day, or those arising from subjects such as literature and history. Problems arising from school and class situations can be discussed even by fairly young pupils and the solutions suggested by them examined. One of the main ways which Kohlberg suggests of improving moral development is by encouraging discussion and the exchanging of ideas, not with the aim of converting everyone to the same decision or of imposing a particular view on them but of breeding in them habits of rational decision making which must include the ability to see the matter from the point of view of others. The interchange of ideas and opinions involves much the same process and probably has much the same effect as was proposed earlier when discussing the development of logical reasoning.

The sort of issues chosen should, as far as possible, arise naturally, with a little help from the teacher, and should be part of the normal learning and teaching rather than feature in special lessons. Even very young children can be encouraged to think about some of the situations arising from stories told to them, or to discuss how they could best help one of their number who is ill or injured, or to solve a real discipline problem. The problem situations should be ones which they can realistically put themselves into, and their ideas should be listened to seriously by teacher and fellow pupils, which in itself is a good example of moral education. For such experience to be of real benefit the teacher's role must be to follow and perhaps suggest new aspects to be looked at, rather than to lead the discussion. He must be very careful not to impose his own solutions or opinions.

As children move towards adolescence they can be faced with increasingly complicated problems, arising mainly from their normal lessons, or school and local issues. History, literature and religious studies and local newspapers are rich sources of discussions arising from questions such as, 'What would you have done, and why?' and 'Was he right or wrong to do what he did? Why?' Some national issues are not beyond the children's powers even though their ideas may not be fully mature. In adolescence the scope and effect of the exchange of ideas widens considerably and, as well as school issues, one can include locally important topics such as 'universal as opposed to selective secondary education,' 'equal pay and opportunities for men and women,' 'the abuse of drugs and alcohol', and 'compulsory control of population movements from rural to urban areas'.

In addition to direct discussion of problem issues, moral development can be encouraged by short, written or impromptu plays created by the pupils, or through role playing which involves one or more children putting forward a particular moral viewpoint, so that the class can discuss it. An imaginative teacher can find many opportunities for involving his pupils in moral issues at suitable levels, and in doing so will not only make his classroom an intellectually stimulating place but will also give his pupils important developmental opportunities.

Teachers in rapidly changing and multi-cultural communities have much the same opportunities and responsibilities as do those in more settled ones, but it is especially important for them to take into account the moral values and practices that exist among the different groups that they teach. When they and most of their pupils have a common experience there is very little difficulty but when they are mixed in cultural and ethnic origin, or even in social class, the teacher will have to be particularly careful that genuine differences in moral customs and traditional values are treated with respect.

A possible dilemma for the teacher himself could occur when his pupils come from a strongly authoritarian environment in which dogma and ideology are instilled at home with great effect. The problem is made greater when he himself cannot accept the beliefs and attitudes. The author, when a very inexperienced teacher, was expected to teach the Book of Genesis to a class of children in a secular school. She did not realise that in the class was a group of children from a local mission which held very strong and fundamentalist views about the absolute and literal truth of the Bible. She approached the story of the Creation by explaining that when people do not understand how something came about they often make up stories to explain it. She quoted some relevant myths about the origin of thunder, for example, and then treated the Creation story as an imaginative explanatory myth which in no way, she thought, diminished the role of God in the process. She was startled at the reaction of both pupils and their parents who, justifiably, accused her of imposing her own views and undermining the religious principles of the children. This was a valuable lesson to learn, and it illustrates the fine line that sometimes exists between encouraging children to learn *how* to think in contrast to *what* to think. The teacher, then, must remember that his main responsibility is to establish the intellectual habits and social skills which will enable his pupils to acquire consistent and suitable standards as a basis on which they can later make sensible and responsible choices and decisions about their own beliefs and behaviour without divorcing them from their own family, community and religious backgrounds.

Application 17

1 Arrange to spend enough time with at least three different groups of children three or four years apart in age (e.g. 8, 12 and 15 years) so that you can tell them in your own words the story of Heinz and the rare drug. Ask them whether Heinz did right to steal the drug and the reasons for their answers. Note how the answers from the three groups differ and decide how far they fit into Kohlberg's categories.

2 With the same, or similar, children ask them to discuss, in small groups, the class and school rules that they would want to change or reject altogether or new ones that they would add, and why. Discuss the results of each group's suggestions with the whole class and ask them to imagine what would be the result of a few of their proposed changes. What differences do you notice between the replies of each age group?

Further reading

There are useful chapters in general educational psychology texts which would extend this chapter, e.g. Sprinthall and Sprinthall (ibid), especially Chapters 8, (p. 151) and 9, (p. 165), Vander Zanden (ibid), Chapter 10, (p. 232).

Read also Wagner and Stevenson, pp. 248 to 279.

CHAPTER ELEVEN

Understanding yourself as a teacher

The emphasis throughout this book has so far been on the learners and how to ensure that their educational needs in the widest sense can be satisfied. We have looked at various aspects of development and how to promote it further and at their psychological needs and how their fulfillment affects both the development and learning processes. From time to time it has been stressed that the teacher's own characteristic attitudes and expectations are important in the educative process but it is now time to focus more particularly on you and what you can do to prepare yourself as a person for the vital influence you will have on the many pupils whom you will eventually teach.

It is hoped that this book has already helped you to develop a concept of children that is based on first hand knowledge and sound information. You should now be less likely to see children as young savages to be tamed, or as blank pages or empty pots to be filled. You should no longer see them as miniature adults, or as incompetent, needing to be organized and ordered in everything that they do. It is very important that a teacher has a realistic perception of children and how they behave and develop because without it he has little chance of being successful in his profession and is in danger of doing harm to many young people, because he has been unable to provide for their real educational development needs.

As well as needing insight into children he must learn to look realistically at himself. For example, we all of us have come from a particular group or social class and our self-concepts include our own idea of our social class or status. It is often the same as that of our parents, though in rapidly changing societies, in which educational opportunity was limited for them, we may see ourselves as having moved upwards from our parents into a higher status group. Our self-concepts also include our personal standards, values and ideas of what is suitable and desirable behaviour. Most teachers come from or have moved into the middle or professional class, whereas their pupils will usually come from all classes, from the lowest to the highest. In Third World and multi-cultural countries the picture can be further complicated by the speed of social and economic change and the inclusion in schools of ethnic and culture groups different from that of the teacher. There is a danger of teachers trying to impose their own values and attitudes on all their pupils, while rejecting or undervaluing traits and attitudes of other groups. The middle class values and virtues most often met in teachers are hard work, punctuality, neatness, cleanliness, deference to authority and acceptance of the rules. These traits are not bad in themselves but are not always the ones which can, or even should, be accepted by all children. Lower class children, or those from different culture groups, may not find it easy to conform to these expectations, the teacher feeling out of sympathy with them, and they with the teacher. Equally, teachers may find it difficult, or not even worthwhile, to talk to and to try to understand the parents of these pupils.

At the other end of the social scale, teachers sometimes think that children from higher social and economic classes are difficult to handle, argumentative and lacking in good manners, and they are sometimes nervous of the parents of such children because of their greater apparent confidence and influence. Unless a teacher makes himself aware of his often hidden attitudes towards and expectations from the full social and cultural range of his pupils, he may find it difficult to build up a classroom climate in which all pupils are equally important. The 'message' that he may convey to a lower esteemed pupil is that they are not very important and are unlikely to make much real educational progress, the result possibly being a poorer self-concept with its educational and other consequences. His anxiety in the presence of higher status pupils may lead to the loss of their confidence in him as their teacher and thus to discipline problems. His tendency to welcome and encourage his own values and expectations in those pupils who already accept them may reduce the opportunities for such children to enrich their personalities and social skills. In many countries school achievement is closely related to the social class of the child. This may in part be accounted for by the capacity of the parents and the home environment to provide a stimulating basis for further learning. It may also stem in part from the teacher's expectations which he derives from his ideas about their capacities and worth.

A teacher's perception of himself as a teacher will also influence his teaching style and the climate of his classroom. As was said before, his self-concept is made up of his major personality traits, his experience of other teachers and his perception of the nature of children and education. Herbert Thelen, in Chicago, drew up a number of different 'models' of teachers from observing them at work. He then asked each teacher to describe how he saw himself as a teacher. When he compared the teachers' own perceptions of themselves with the ones that he had built up from watching them, he found that they fitted closely with each other. He describes, for example, the teacher who sees himself as a sort of Socrates, after the ancient Greek philosopher whose teaching method was to probe the learner's thinking by a continuous series of questions which he hoped would lead them to clarify their ideas. There is some merit in the use of this technique but it has limited value as a major method because it is more concerned with the process of debate than with arriving at conclusions and deciding on actions. Such a teacher sees himself as the source of all wisdom and knowledge, with the result that he keeps the focus of class activity on himself, directing the pupils' thinking into his own channels.

Then there is the so-called 'town manager', who runs his class rather as though it were a public meeting at which everyone is encouraged to contribute, he himself playing very little part in determining the direction that the discussion will take. Again there is a place for a certain amount of democracy in the classroom but not with the result of haphazard progress following thoughts of the moment rather than a course planned to coincide with and build on the children's needs. This teaching style is also more likely to satisfy the teacher's rather than the pupils' requirements.

A more comprehensive approach to the role of the teacher is used by someone whom Thelen calls the 'apprentice master', who sees himself as a model for his pupils to copy. He tries to be all things to his pupils, teacher, friend, father, colleague and boss. Certainly there are times when a teacher has to fill roles such as these but there is a danger of the individuality of the pupils being swallowed up because of the strength of his teacher's idea of himself as being a worthy model for them to copy.

A much more common type of teacher Thelen calls the 'army

general'. He is one who lays down the law and demands instant and complete obedience from his pupils. He may or may not also be Thelen's 'business man' who prides himself on being thoroughly well organized and completely efficient. Teachers do indeed need to be well organized and efficient but with the major purpose of providing a suitable atmosphere for the real work of the children to take place, whereas the business man teacher likes efficiency for its own sake. He cannot tolerate or understand that the young are not basically efficient or well organized. He also tends to regard lists of marks, class orders, charts, etc., as good pictures of his pupils, forgetting that human beings are much more than mechanical symbols.

As was noted before, all these teachers adopt methods which are more likely to satisfy themselves than to provide a rich learning and developmental environment for their pupils. What is really needed is a 'model' for an 'educator of children' in which the teacher builds his own concept of an ideal teacher largely from his knowledge of the needs and potential of the pupils and the educational purposes that he must help them to achieve. But it is important to remember that there is no single ideal teaching style and every teacher must develop one which best suits his personality while at the same time fulfilling the real needs of the pupils. Some will be more authoritarian, or democratic, or confident, or permissive than others, with real benefit to the children whom they influence. It is only when the style which a teacher is able to develop and use with competence and confidence is widely and consistently different from the pupils' real needs that harm may follow.

It is the responsibility of every teacher, then, to look closely at himself from time to time to see what sort of teacher he seems to be and how far he is able to achieve personal satisfaction as well as overall success in the classroom. If he has been able to build up realistic perceptions of the nature of children and their development, and the nature of his responsibilities towards them, and uses these as bases on which to plan his teaching and classroom procedures, the chances are that he has established a self-concept of himself as a teacher which is effective.

Application 18

Work with a group of three or four fellow students, each one taking it in turn to teach at least two prepared lessons with different classes, watched by the rest of the group. Make a check list such as the one opposite, each observer completing it independently of the rest of the group. The student who is being observed should also complete it about himself. Award a mark of one to five for each trait listed, the mark of one indicating only little evidence of the trait and five indicating strong evidence of it. The marks of two, three and four are given for levels in between the extremes.

Once the check lists have been completed take it in turns to discuss constructively each other's assessments, noting the successful as well as the unsuccessful facets and suggesting useful modifications. There may be other traits which you think should be added to the list which would extend one's understanding of oneself.

1 Were the pupils mostly:
relaxed?
busy?
certain?
trusting of the teacher?
resentful?
noisy?
seat-bound (i.e. unable or unprepared to move from their seats)?
willing to seek help from the teacher?
willing to seek help from fellow pupils?
willing to volunteer the answers to questions?
willing to offer ideas?
spontaneous in their reactions?
tense?
under-occupied?
confused?
suspicious of the teacher?
cheerful?
very quiet?
ready to laugh?
ready to move from their seats when necessary?
reluctant to seek help from the teacher?
reluctant to seek help from a fellow pupil?
reluctant to answer questions?
reluctant to offer ideas?

2 Was the teacher mostly;
at ease and relaxed?
patient?
helpful to individuals?
confident?
tense?
irritable?
liable to ignore individuals?
diffident?
tolerant of working noise?
impatient of noise?
in overall control?

friendly to the children?
disorganized?
able to smile?
able to laugh?
tolerant of the children's laughter?
looking grim?

All work has its own stresses and tensions which have implications for the health of the worker, the teacher as much as any other, and it is important for those who are starting out on their careers to know some of the possibilities. On the physical side, there is the possibility of an initial susceptibility to colds and other minor infections resulting from the unaccustomed exposure to concentrated germs in a classroom. But most teachers soon build up a relative immunity to these ills. Of more importance for teachers is what is often called *mental health*, which is a much more positive concept than merely the absence of mental disease. There is no evidence that teachers are more subject to real mental illness than are the rest of the population, but they are often subjected to pressures and stresses which may in some circumstances drain their reserves of energy, reduce their effectiveness as teachers and limit their satisfaction from their work. Some of the pressures come as part of the job itself while others can occur when external circumstances prevent them from doing all that they would like to do.

As is almost always the case when considering the possible reactions of human beings to more or less similar sets of circumstances, there are considerable individual differences in the way that stress can be withstood, some people perhaps being born more able than others to stand up to pressure. While none of us can alter our physical inheritance it is possible to reduce the likelihood of suffering from stress and to control its effects when it cannot be avoided. First of all, stress is felt when the realities of a situation do not match one's expectations, although most people eventually manage to adjust their expectations to fit the reality. In teaching it quite often happens that newly-qualified teachers in their first teaching post find that, despite their experience during training, they do not understand the full range of their responsibilities. This, combined with the inevitable anxieties of starting in a new career in an unfamiliar school among unknown colleagues, can cause loss of self confidence and even real distress. Fortunately most come through this period safely but it is a help to a new teacher to realise that his initial experiences and reactions are very common and that they will soon be replaced by happier feelings.

The iniation into teaching can be greatly eased if the school Head and staff remember their own beginnings and take special steps to welcome the newcomer and to make sure that he knows about the organization of the school and the necessary administrative routines. Some schools attach each newcomer to a sympathetic established staff member who will ease him into his work. The new teacher, too, must be ready to take the initiative and be prepared to ask questions and seek advice when necessary. The early attitudes shown and impressions given by a new staff member to the existing members are important, since both overconfidence and lack of confidence and can sometimes start the important inter-relationships on the wrong foot.

Occasionally people become teachers because they unconsciously see this as a way of staying in a familiar safe environment, without having to risk exposure to the wider world. They move from school (as pupils) to college (as students) and back to school (as teachers) without any real break. Such people, because of their unusually strong need for security and stability, may find that teaching is not, after all, the comfortable haven that they were seeking, especially when they are challenged by large classes, reluctant pupils, demanding parents, heavy timetables and so on. Unless they can overcome their immaturity they are unlikely to be happy and successful because, above all, teachers need to be mature and self-reliant, focussing their efforts on the pupils and the school rather than on satisfying their own inner needs. This is not to say that all entrants to the teaching profession who do not have a significant break in the school-college-school circle are immature and seeking security. Indeed, a majority of successful teachers take that route. It is, however, important that trainee teachers and those intending to make it their career, look at their own motives honestly to make sure that they really are seeking a profession and career and not a safe retreat.

Another danger which could threaten a teacher's professional and personal life is that of becoming too involved with the children and with the job, with the possible result of losing their sense of balance so that trivial things grow out of proportion. Everyone, and a teacher more than most, needs a full and varied personal life outside school and career, so that they can keep abreast of events and developments in the wider community and keep their work in perspective. It is possible and necessary to combine dedication to the job with a separate and adult personal existence outside school. To achieve this one must make sure that one has time, free of school responsibilities, to pursue an absorbing hobby or interest. It is important, too, for teachers to develop and maintain contacts with adults in their community who are not teachers. School holidays are not necessarily the luxury that some people imagine. Much preparation for the work of the following term should be done in these breaks, but there is also need for activities which are truly recreational at an adult level.

If, despite the warnings and his efforts, a teacher finds himself persistently and increasingly unhappy, anxious, tense, short-tempered and reluctant to teach, it is important that he do something about it both for his own and his pupils' sakes. All teachers at times experience these feelings but they are usually balanced out by the satisfactions, successes and joyful moments. When this balance is lacking he needs to analyse very carefully what the cause of the unhappiness might be. It may be fairly simple, in that he is not planning realistically and in enough detail to ensure that his lessons go smoothly. A reorganization of his approach may be all that is necessary. Perhaps he does not have enough interests and satisfaction in his life outside the job, with the result that he expects too much from his work and is disappointed. Perhaps he really does have a combination of large classes, heavy timetables, administrative responsibilities and poor equipment so that he cannot give time and energy to the real work of teaching and thus feels frustrated. In such a case, serious discussion with his Head and staff colleagues may help lighten his load and boost his morale, as well as help him to establish more realistic priorities in his work and recreation. Finally, perhaps he is, after all, in the wrong profession, or the wrong part of it, and more drastic action on his part is needed, either by transferring elsewhere in the education system or even by changing to another line of work altogether. Certainly the individual who really enjoys his work, derives satisfaction from it, has happy relationships with his pupils and colleagues and at the same time leads an adult existence apart from his work, is the sort of teacher that all systems require. If the excitement and joy which teaching can provide do not exist for him, then something is seriously wrong and drastic action is needed.

There are some special stresses more likely to be experienced by teachers in rapidly developing countries. For example, the teaching facilities and resources in rural and remoter areas may be limited and classes unduly large, or have wide age ranges.

Ingenuity and imagination can overcome this, especially if one remembers that, in addition to the essential skills related to literacy and numeracy, the development of the sense of curiosity and wonder and powers of observation, which are important educational responsibilities, can take place in the children's own natural environment. Local plants, animals, geographical features, materials and the wisdom and folklore of the local people can all be used to very great effect. Of more importance in such circumstances, is the possibility that the teacher may be one of very few people in the district with much education, and he may find little social and intellectual stimulation. He may even be from a different ethnic or cultural group, which could limit his initial acceptance by the local population. The best antidote to the isolation and loneliness that he might feel is not to withdraw from the area at the earliest opportunity but, because of his awareness of the situation, to go out of his way to get involved with the local people, who may be just as wary of him as he is of them. The parents of his pupils are a good starting point, making the school something of a focal point in the village life and helping them to feel that they have a part to play in the education of their children. Despite the earlier warnings about the possible effects of becoming so totally involved in one's job that one has no adult and independent existence of one's own, it is more important to avoid social and intellectual isolation by, for example, starting adult literacy classes, or organizing activities for young people. Teachers who are prepared to take an active part in a local community can make an important contribution to its development which can give a good deal of personal satisfaction.

Finally, a word needs to be said about the continuing education and professional development of the teacher. The successful completion of an initial training course before or at an early stage in one's teaching career should be seen both by teachers and by educational authorities as precisely that, *initial* training. In the past, employers have often regarded a recognized professional certificate or diploma, and some practical experience, as sufficient to ensure that a teacher can keep abreast of new developments in educational tecnhiques and philosophies, as well as social and cultural changes, and thus not only retain but extend his teaching competence throughout his career. Such an attitude assumes firstly, that teachers are motivated to read widely throughout their careers about new approaches to their job and new information about child development and the subject matter to be taught.

It also assumes that school Heads and educational advisers have sufficient contact with teachers to stimulate them to continue their professional development beyond their immediate classroom experience. Quite often this is indeed the case, but research in many countries shows that too high a proportion of teachers rarely read around their profession or take positive steps to renew and extend their expertise, with the result that, once they have reached stability and a reasonable level of classroom performance, they become reluctant to change their established attitudes and methods. Each year that passes repeats their past methods and adds little to their experience. There are many reasons for this, such as lack of time free from the problems of keeping up with the immediate demands of the job, or lack of an external incentive to change. Whatever the reasons, both teacher and pupils are likely to be the losers, the former in that, though he has made his professional life comfortable and safe, he may no longer find it stimulating and exciting, and the latter in that they may be deprived of important educational experiences, including contact with an enthusiastic teacher. All that a book such as this can do is to urge intending teachers to resolve to continue their own educational development, through reading, staff room discussion and the attendance at vacation and in-service courses where they exist.

The author has had considerable experience with mature teachers who attend developmental courses. Many admit to enrolling in the first place because they saw it as a stage in career advancement, which indeed it often is. Almost universally, however, they soon begin to feel a renewed sense of purpose in their career which they had not realized had become so routine and unadventurous. Once the course is over some have gone on to establish discussion and research groups in their own home districts in order to continue the processes begun on their course. While only relatively few teachers have regular opportunities to take in-service courses, most have access to books or to individuals who will help to maintain their interest and improve their knowledge and expertise, which can do much not only to make them better teachers but also to enrich their lives. The teacher who is also a lifelong learner is the teaching profession's most needed asset.

Further reading

Look in the index of general texts for chapters headed something like 'Teaching: the Personal Dimension' as in Sprinthall and Sprinthall (ibid)

Chapter 14, p. 281 and 'The Teacher', as in Vander Zanden, Chapter 12, p. 288.
Are there any local studies about what makes good teachers?

CHAPTER TWELVE

Educational assessment

As we have seen, educational psychology has an important contribution to make in helping teachers both to make clear the main purposes of their job and to develop teaching methods which will achieve those purposes. No educational programme or teaching plan is complete if it does not also include reliable and valid ways of discovering how far it is successful and where it falls short of its goals. It will be noticed that the emphasis in the last sentence is on assessing the success of the teaching programme and methods used, rather than on the achievements of the learners. Of course, in most circumstances, the only way of finding out whether a teaching programme has been successful is by measuring, or at least identifying, the effect that it has on the learners, but it is important to emphasise to teachers at an early stage of their careers that virtually all testing, examination and other analytic activities ought primarily to be assessing the *effects of the total learning experience* on the pupils. If it has not had the intended effect then the teacher must look back over the methods used and what the learner was expected to do, so as to identify what went wrong. He must also decide, on the basis of the evaluation and analysis, what the learner needs to make further progress. In a very real way, tests, examinations and other methods of assessment are saying as many things about the teacher as about the pupil. To use them solely as labels to attach to pupils is to overlook an important part of their function.

Evaluation and assessment in education takes many forms. They include the quick, often informal testing during the course of a lesson which is done to check that the important points are so far understood. They also include the more formal exercises, tests, examinations and reports which form a large part of a teacher's responsibilities. The form which the testing takes must be chosen in the light of the function that it has to serve, though some procedures may fulfill more than one purpose.

Major purposes of educational assessment

1 Measurement of attainment

This is the most widely needed and used form of assessment and aims at discovering how much the learner has actually learned from his lessons or the level of knowledge, understanding and skill that he already has at the beginning of a new area of study. This second aim is to give the teacher a basis on which to build the new learning programme. In order to be able to assess attainment the teacher must be very specific about what the learning objectives of his programmes are. These must include not only the facts and skills that the learners should acquire but also what they should be able to do with those facts and skills when they have learned them. Earlier in this book it was emphasised that preparation of any learning unit or lesson must include a statement of objectives, preferably in a form something like this:

By the end of the lesson the pupils should be able (for example):
to tell the story accurately in their own words;
to give three reasons for the migration southwards of the Bantu tribes;
to explain what would happen if a sealed glass tube full of water were frozen, and why;
to plan a succession of crops to be planted on sandy loam soil at an altitude of 5000 feet (1000 metres) in an East African Monsoon climate, giving valid reasons for the proposals;
to make a simple plan of the classroom showing the relative positions of the door, windows and the teacher's table;
to demonstrate, on a relief map, the best transport route from a planned copper mine to the seaport, explaining reasons for the choice.

Such statements contain in them the means of assessing the pupils learning, even though they are rarely considered to be formal tests, and are educationally and psychologically the most important ways of assessing attainment. They help the teacher to know immediately which pupils need help and which aspects of the topic need further work. They give immediate information about his progress to the learner himself and a chance to develop his self confidence and sense of mastery. They also give a chance for immediate correction and further explanation where needed. If the objectives are well analysed and designed to make sure that there is understanding and application of knowledge rather than mere collections of facts, they are important guidelines in lesson preparation and will make the choice of teaching methods easier. They will also make for better teaching and longer lasting learning. In this sense, then, assessment of attainment is an integral part of the teaching and learning processes.

In addition to the built-in assessment of attainment described above there is also need for periodic evaluation of a whole learning unit, or completed section of a topic, both to see how successfully the parts have been linked into a whole and to assess how well the pupils have remembered what they have learned. The same functions as those described in the previous paragraph are served by such attainment tests, and they also often serve as reinforcers of the earlier learning. To be efficient they should be closely linked to the longer term objectives of the part of the curriculum that they test and be designed to assess understanding and application rather than simple recall.

Many schools require end of term or end of year tests and examinations and it is important to be sure of the purpose of such assessments and the uses to which the results will be put, so that the most appropriate procedures can be selected. The principal purposes are, firstly to find out the progress in that subject that each pupil has made. Secondly, some teachers, parents and pupils see the results as a way of evaluating the progress of each pupil in comparison with all the other pupils, so that an order of merit can be drawn up. The use to which such information is put needs to be considered very carefully. Thirdly, end of term or end of year tests and examinations are seen as motivators both to the teacher and the pupil, in that they are likely to put greater effort into their teaching and learning because they know that their achievements will be known to others. Fourthly, they may be used as bases for selection into later classes, streams or learning programmes, implying that it is possible to predict future performance from the results. Fifthly, they can be used to enable teachers to identify areas where more or different teaching is needed.

Because of the wide range of purposes and the important decisions which may be made on the basis of information yielded, it is vital that, if formal end of year or end of course assessments are required, the test procedures used will actually give the information hoped for. Unfortunately it is a difficult task, especially for the class teacher, to achieve. Usually the best that can be done by teachers who are required to produce their own tests is firstly, to specify in as much detail as possible the learning objectives of the course concerned. On the basis of these he must then devise questions and exercises which will allow the pupils to demonstrate that they have achieved these objectives, emphasising the *application* of facts and skills rather than their mechanical reproduction. Inevitably they will be able to test directly only a fairly small part of the work covered so that the selection of the most important aspects will be vital. Well prepared teacher tests can be used to summarise achievement and focus on both teaching and learning, but by their very nature, the results should be used cautiously if one wants to draw conclusions about the relative progress of individuals or use them as predictors of future success. There is a further danger inherent in formal examinations for both pupils and teachers. They may mistakenly see the purpose of education as being to pass examinations, so that they focus their learning and teaching on test requirements rather than on real educational needs.

To summarise the position as regards formal end of term or end of year testing, it can be said that it has a place, provided that the test requirements arise out of the real learning objectives which themselves should emphasise understanding and applicability of the knowledge and skills involved. If used to reinforce and summarise learning and to be a basis for further learning they can have some value if they genuinely cover the essential ground. On the other hand, if what is needed is an assessment of individual pupils which will allow reliable decisions to be made about an individual's future educational placement, more information is needed. This additional information should include, at the very least, a detailed record of the continuing progress made by the pupil throughout the course. This aspect of assessment will be discussed in more detail later, as will some of the available techniques for testing and assessing.

A further point to make about assessing learning progress concerns the practice in some schools of having several parallel streams of pupils being taught the same syllabus by different teachers. Often a common test or examination is set at the end of the year for all the classes. The reasons for this include the need to make sure that that all the pupils are learning the same material in more or less the same way, with the additional possibility that one may be able to compare the professional competence of the different teachers involved. The construction of such tests should be the result of much co-operation within the teaching team, which should in any case have decided among themselves the detailed objectives at the outset of their course, as well as the major examination techniques to be used, if not the actual questions and tasks. In some schools, more often in primary ones where the teaching specialises less in subjects, the Head himself may set the end of year tests. Fortunately, this is now a fairly rare practice because it has its own dangers, not least because it implies that the Head does not trust his staff members' professional competence.

The last form of attainment testing to be considered here is that which is undertaken by a body outside the school and intended to be used for large numbers of pupils in many different schools. Under this heading come the examination procedures often adopted in education systems where there is need to select only a proportion of pupils for a further stage of their education, such as at the end of the primary school. There are still some countries that have not yet managed to provide good quality secondary schools for all pupils so need some means of selecting those who are most likely to benefit from further schooling.

More widely influential are the so-called public examinations which are used to give overall assessments of a pupil's school achievement, often in the form of a School Leaving Certificate, a Certificate of Secondary Education or a General Certificate of Education. The Certificate, which usually records the level of attainment in a number of school subjects, is widely used by education selectors and prospective employers to help them to decide whether the individual applicant is knowledgeable and well-educated enough to enter higher education courses or to undertake certain work. The setting of such examinations is highly skilled and professional work and involves not only the setting of questions and devising activities which will test the achievement of a comprehensive range of curriculum objectives but also of ensuring that the many different examiners and script markers work to the same standard. The standard of achievement has to be established not only for each subject or paper but care has to be taken to ensure that the levels expected in one curriculum subject are comparable with those of all other subjects. For example, a first class pass in mathematics should somehow make the same demands as a first class pass in history, technical drawing or home economics. The proportions of candidates expected to achieve at each grade of pass or fail are usually decided beforehand on a statistical basis, which adds to the problems of the examiners. As well as the difficulties of setting and marking public examinations there is the need to ensure that the teachers whose pupils will eventually become examination candidates know well in advance the syllabus which will be examined and the examiners' objectives, so that they can set their own teaching objectives accordingly.

A further problem is that some less experienced education authorities in newer countries gear at least the academic aspects of their secondary school curriculum to the examination bodies of other countries, or to one established jointly by a group of neighbouring countries. Fortunately, the professionally reputable examination bodies make sure that the syllabuses which are examined are relevant to the needs of the customers and they link closely with them. The advantages of public examinations of the sort described above include the establishment of a common expectation of an objective standard so that the achievement of individuals from different schools and education systems can be compared. They can provide a standard of performance at which schools can aim, since some people think that this is the most effective way of motivating both pupils and teachers to higher attainment. They also have drawbacks, both educational and social, of which parents, employers and educators need to be aware. For example, the public examination system has had a great influence on some educational philosophies and curricula, even though this is not their real purpose. Because the possession of educational certificates is so influential, many people see the main purpose of secondary schooling to be to ensure that as many as possible of its pupils eventually obtain them. The curriculum content is sometimes overweighted with examination subjects and the syllabuses rigidly interpreted in terms of the examination requirements, both teachers and pupils seeing any deviation from them as endangering their futures. Less confident teachers are reluctant to try adventurous and imaginative methods of pupil activity, adopting instead a didactic, bookish approach, varied by frequent completion of exercises from past examination papers. The author has often heard experienced teachers say, 'I have no time to educate my pupils. I have to get them through their examinations'. Opportunities for the development of intellectual and personal qualities and skills may thus be reduced.

Before leaving the subject of attainment assessment via the process of certification, it is important to remember that, despite the school's and pupil's best efforts, such factors as personality, anxiety level and health can affect performance in any formal examination so that the results are not necessarily a reflection of the realities. Even more significant, however, are the psychological and social effects of the procedure. Public examinations are usually structured to spread out the results more or less along a curve of normal distribution described earlier (see Chap 8). This means that everyone's results can be seen as almost an order of merit, giving important messages to individuals about their worthiness and ability. In a society in which school results and examination grades are important they may, and probably will be over emphasised when evaluating an individual and his status, giving false hope to some and despair to others. It could be said that public examinations are a form of *social engineering* by which individuals are allocated a certain status in society and granted or denied certain opportunities. In older countries this aspect is now diminishing, though probably too slowly. In some newly developing countries, for understandable historic and economic reasons, the danger still exists and it is important for all those involved in education to put correct interpretations on examination results and implement the wider educational perspectives which every country needs. As we shall see later, there are alternative methods of assessment which can yield a more comprehensive picture of the individual concerned and in doing so be less likely to over influence curricula and teaching objectives adversely.

2 Diagnosis

We have already touched on the use of testing procedures to identify, or diagnose, learning problems on an individual and group basis. Indeed, only on rare occasions should tests or assessments be used purely for administrative purposes with no diagnostic element. Even public examinations can, by analysing the spread of results, give information about the relative strengths and weaknesses of the teaching and learning of different subjects in different schools and by different groups of candidates. Of more immediate concern to teachers is how to identify, quickly and accurately, specific areas of learning difficulty that individuals and groups have. For example, there may be children who have problems in learning to read, for which there may be many causes. The individual may not be mature enough mentally to make much progress at the early stages of reading, or he may not have enough knowledge of the written symbols or the techniques of word analysis, or he may have developed a poor or inappropriate general approach to reading. Until the real cause, or causes, of reading failure are discovered, attempts to remove them by using suitable remedial techniques could be less than successful. Similarly in mathematics, at almost any stage in school some pupils may have fallen behind in their attainment because they have not fully understood an essential intermediate concept. Examples can be drawn from many educational areas where there is need for a more detailed analysis and diagnosis than can be done by ordinary classroom activities.

The sensitive and experienced teacher can, with patience, often devise simple classroom tests which will help him to identify particular problems. In reading, for example, he can watch closely and make notes of the commonest errors, which may give a clue to the reader's needs. Once this is done, he can plan a special programme of exercises and activities designed to make good the lack. Similarly, in mathematics and number work, if he understands the concepts and techniques which are fundamental to the learning of more complex processes, he can easily make simple tests to discover where the basic knowledge is missing. Diagnosis in education, then, is an important but everyday function of the teacher and is part of the ongoing assessment and evaluation procedures for all learning.

There are times, however, when something more is needed because the teacher's ability and the available facilities are insufficient or the problem too complex for simple measures. Diagnosis in cases like this must start with the teacher realising that a pupil needs special help. Too many teachers, probably because of lack of time and pressure of work, accept as inevitable the special problems that some learners have, and let them struggle on their own. Such individuals usually fall further behind, which makes the problem even worse. Research shows that this has been the case in many of the unacceptably high numbers of poor readers who are in the older forms and among school leavers. Too few secondary schools check the reading ability of those pupils who are making slow progress in other areas. Reading is a subject in which early diagnosis of difficulties is important since poor reading is major cause of poor general achievement.

There is available a number of published diagnostic tests, most of which are simple to use by the teacher, though it is essential that they follow the instructions meticulously. The tests usually consist of a systematically graded series of exercises designed to pinpoint the particular process, concepts or skills which are not adequately learned. Once the area of difficultly has been identified, it is the teacher's responsibility to take the learner back to that point and build up learning again from there. Obviously, the sooner such a diagnosis is made the better, because it becomes increasingly difficult in most ordinary classrooms for the teacher to give time to those who are seriously retarded. The subjects in which published diagnostic tests are most easily available are reading and number work, since these have a fairly easily identifiable progression of knowledge and skills which must be followed in their logical order. Published diagnostic tests in other educational areas do not seem to have much real use in most classrooms.

Most schools and education authorities have some facilities for expert diagnosis of learning problems though in many countries which are still struggling to provide basic education for increasing numbers, the facilities are very limited. It is important that teachers know what facilities are available to them and the criteria for their use. They can then decide from their own initial diagnosis what steps can be taken in their own classroom to improve learning and what use they can make of other outside services. As with all evaluation and assessment, diagnosis and analysis are ongoing commitments of all teachers and a vital part of the teaching process. It is a state of mind and should be part of the teacher's concept of education and his role in it and not an occasional item used only when serious and apparently intractable learning problems have arisen.

3 Assessment of abilities and aptitudes

In assessing some pupils, especially those who still fail to make progress in their learning despite everything possible being done to help them, it would be useful to know something about their potential capacity for learning. If such a person is shown to be incapable of learning at the level at which he finds himself then decisions can be made about the best course of action for him. The sort of testing procedures likely to be needed in a case such as this can only be undertaken by a professional psychologist who will decide what tests to administer and what the results mean. This is not the place to go into details about such tests since the classroom teacher is concerned with the meaning of the information that the psychologist can give him and what action to take in the individual case. All that needs to be said here is that if there is any doubt about what the results of a specialist examination mean the teacher should, probably through the school Head, seek further information. A cautionary word should be said if the report from the psychologist places much emphasis on the individual's Intelligence Quotient or Scholastic Aptitude figure. By itself, such a figure does not tell one much about someone with learning problems and more information should be sought. For example, one would need to know whether a low score was the result of poor motivation, or limited language ability or persistent ill-health or any of the many possible causes in addition to genuinely poor intellectual potential.

In new and rapidly growing education systems, the psychological services available may still be limited and the tests which can be used with confidence few in number. Consequently, more responsibility falls on the teachers. An experienced and sensitive teacher can often identify, fairly accurately at least, some of the causes of learning problems and even when these are extensive, he should be slow to reject the poor individual unless he is sure that there is a better alternative for him elsewhere.

Some techniques of educational assessment

Some of these have already been mentioned earlier in the chapter but it is worth spending time on describing and illustrating the more important ones in some detail, while emphasising that whichever method, or methods are selected, consideration must first be given to the purposes of the assessment and the learning objectives of the material which is being evaluated.

1 Teacher's subjective observations

All teachers, either consciously or unconsciously, make *subjective* judgements and decisions about their pupils. By subjective assessments we mean the conclusions that are drawn about the individual, his capacity, personality and behaviour from many different, small clues which we may notice over a period of time. It is often difficult to be certain exactly what clues have contributed to our opinion of an individual. Our subconscious minds have absorbed them and tried to make sense of them so that we can, to some extent, tell in advance how he will behave in a given situation; we would be surprised when our predictions are not fulfilled. Analysis of this sort is an important aspect of human behaviour and interaction in all aspects of life. In the classroom, the process assumes particular importance, not least because of the influence of the 'self-fulfilling prophecy' which has already been discussed. It is not being suggested here that there is no place for subjective assessment of pupils. But care must be taken by teachers to see that their opinions about the children whom they teach are as free from prejudice as possible so that they really add something constructive to the educational plans for, and expectations from, each individual. The main dangers to be avoided include being influenced by irrelevant factors, accepting other people's (especially other teachers') opinions unthinkingly, and 'labelling' a child with a generalisation ('lazy', 'clever', 'unco-operative', etc) and then 'seeing' that trait in the child even when it is not being shown. Research has shown for example, that some teachers' subjective assessments of pupils are influenced by the smartness or otherwise of their clothing, the status of their parents, their religious and ethnic affiliations and so on. Others tend to assume that all children from the same family will show the same traits, thus blinding them to the real individual differences. Many a child has been handicapped by being unfavourably compared to another member of his family.

Subjective assessment of a pupil's progress and performance, then, is a universal process and teachers must make conscious efforts to ensure that their observations and conclusions about their pupils are supported by evidence of what is really there. Because subjective assessment is liable to distortion, it is essential that in addition as much *objective* evaluation as possible is done so as to get as close as possible to the real person.

2 Teacher-made tests

Some of the subjectivity is taken out of the assessment of pupils' learning by the use of some of the many testing methods that teachers can devise. These range from quick oral questioning to written and practical exercises given in class or as homework, to see how far the learning objectives have been achieved. When making their own tests, teachers should decide on the sort of information that they them want to reveal. If they need to know how well a practical skill has been acquired, the test must be of that skill. The author well remembers that in the school where she was a pupil, progress in needlework was tested through written examinations, which asked for descriptions and diagrams of various sewing techniques, hems, patches, etc. Since she was notoriously the least competent needlewoman in the class, it was ironic, and unjust, that she almost invariably scored the highest marks for this subject, until a new teacher was appointed who had a more realistic idea of what competence in needlework is.

Test questions may seek simple recall of information, examples of which include:

what is the altitude of Mount Kilimanjaro?

describe the major steps in the growing of cassava;

write down the correct spelling of the following words (given orally).

Such questions have a place but should rarely appear on formal tests or examination papers because they should be part of the ongoing learning experience, the knowledge being reinforced at the time. More demanding questions seek evidence that the knowledge is understood and can be applied, the pupils being asked more than just to remember what the teacher or the text book said. For example, even young children could be told a short story about a family, giving arithmetical information about their ages, a shopping trip and so on, the story describing a situation which is familiar to them. They are then asked to pretend that they are the teacher and, using the given figures, to make up, say, three sums for each of the four rules, and then work out the answers. Such a task does much more than test their competence at mechanical arithmetic, in that it probes their understanding of the concepts underlying the four rules. Tests of this sort can be done by younger children in an informal, practical way, using apparatus if necessary. The same principle can be applied even to higher mathematics pupils and to other subjects.

Another variant of the technique involves the use of blank maps, or diagrams of local features, or laboratory apparatus, perhaps accompanied by a brief written explanation by the pupil. A wide range of literary skills, from simple comprehension by young children to the higher levels of poetic criticism can be assessed by giving them the actual book from which to work. Independent study and research skills, and many other abilities, can be assessed through what are known as 'open book' examinations. There are, then, many ways in which an imaginative teacher can test and assess learning, in addition to the traditional, written, descriptive or essay-type questions. The selection of the techniques and the demands to be made of the examinee must be determined by the learning objectives that are to be tested, which will in turn depend on the clarity and suitability of their original analysis.

Having decided on how to assess the learning which should have taken place, it is important to make sure that the teacher's marking and evaluation of the results is efficient and not too time consuming. A major drawback to essay-type tests and exercises is the sheer volume of words which it may be necessary to sift through to see whether all the important points have been made. Then, research has shown that two different people marking the same essay often come up with very different results. Even more surprising is the fact that the same person making the same piece of work on different occasions may give quite different assessments, especially when the question was not precisely worded and the information about the examinee that it was meant to yield was not carefully analysed in advance. Consideration should also be given in advance to the relative weight of marks that different aspects of the test answers will carry. For example, the ability to handle complex ideas and to show originality within the required area should be given more marks than the simple basic answers which suggest that they represent the limits of the examinee's understanding.

Teacher-made tests, then, are important contributors to learning and its assessment, and require more thought and skill than is often given to them. Not only should they test the real learning objectives economically and accurately but also be interesting in themselves so that the pupils are motivated to do their best. If they can also contribute to their learning, so much the better.

3 Objective tests

These are tests which are worded so that the questions will bring the exact answers that the teacher wants, which makes for fairer and easier marking and can give good opportunities for relating learning objectives to test questions. It is easy to test recall and recognition of straightforward knowledge through such means but less easy to word the questions so that they will show that the concept or the principle to be tested has been understood. Many public examining bodies use at least some objective tests in their processes. Often they compile a large collection of possible questions to test their learning objectives and try them out to see how well they do what is required of them. The good questions are carefully graded and stored in a 'bank', so that at a later date selections from the store can be put together to form a new objective test.

The form in which the questions are put and the ways of

answering them vary. The commonest is known as *multiple choice*, in which the question is asked and four or five possible answers given. The candidate has to select the best one, either by ticking it or by putting a symbol in a certain place. If there are several alternative answers there is less chance of the candidate getting the right one by guesswork. The following are examples of multiple choice questions.

Choose the right word to complete the following sentences, putting its number in the box.

The capital of Nigeria is: ☐
1   Lusaka
2   Cairo
3   Lagos
4   Harare
5   Kano

This is a very simple recall question. The next one is more demanding.

The speed with which a pendulum swings is dependent on: ☐
1   its weight
2   the length of its arm
3   the altitude
4   the range of its swing
5   none of these

Another method is for several statements to be made and the examinee asked to decide whether each is true or false.
Decide whether each statement below is true or false and underline your choice.
1   The daylight hours in the summer decrease the nearer one goes to the North or South Pole. True/false
2   On the Equator the days and nights are of equal length throughout the year. True/false
3   The prevailing winds at the Equator are from east to west. True/false

The effects of guessing can be reduced by including several questions on the same point but asked in different ways.

A third technique is to give two lists of questions, statements or words which have to be rearranged so as to match each other, as follows.

Put the number of the word or phrase in the second list which correctly completes sentences which begin with each phrase in the first list.

List 1
Bilharzia is caused by _____
Malaria is caused by _____
Dysentery is caused by _____
Measles is caused by _____
Trachoma is caused by _____

List 2
1 flies.
2 drinking contaminated water.
3 contact with water infested with the parasite.
4 mosquitoes.
5 germs from an infected person.

Another method used in objective tests is to give unlabelled diagrams, the examinee being asked to mark certain features on it. For example, understanding of some mechanical principles can be demonstrated, as follows.

Which way does wheel X move when wheel Y is turned in a clockwise direction? Show the direction by putting an arrow below wheel X.

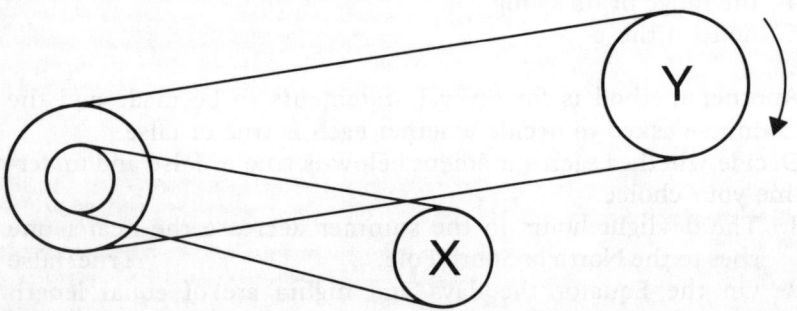

In a book such as this it is not possible to give more than a few examples of objective test techniques. Further reading is suggested at the end of the chapter. Although class teachers should be encouraged to experiment with their own objective tests, they are not always a substitute for the tasks and exercises that demand more positive and original responses from their pupils. Even the best objective tests tend to make use of passive knowledge and can give very little scope for the originality and independent ideas which should also feature in the assessment process. On the other hand, pupils may well be asked at some stage to complete objective tests and it is important that they have a chance to become familiar with the techniques involved.

4 Continuous assessment

The most valuable form of educational assessment which teachers can make is usually known as *continuous assessment*. This is an approach which involves the keeping of a record of progress and performance in key class exercises and tests. It should be much more than a mere record of the marks obtained and should include comments on learning difficulties encountered, particular strengths and talents and any other relevant information. The records should also be enriched by the teacher's comments and observations. The aim is to compile, for each child, a full and progressive picture of his educational development which can follow him on his way through the education system. It has the immediate advantage of ensuring that the teacher has to spend at least several minutes each week pondering over and assessing each pupil in his class, thus reducing the danger of anyone being overlooked. It has the longer term benefit of ultimately giving a fairly comprehensive picture of a range of abilities, skills and personal traits for each individual so that decisions about educational and vocational choices can be made on firm bases. It is important that the continuous assessment and the individual records be more informative than a series of ticks on a chart. Records of this sort, still all too common, say very little about the human being to whom they refer. It is the author's contention that a constructive and conscientiously kept continuous assessment made by sensitive and aware teachers should play at least as important a part in any school certification process as the current formal examination results, and should be available to the pupil himself, the parents and others in the education system.

5 School reports

A final word needs to be said about school reports. It is every parent's right to have an honest and understandable account of his children's progress and personal development. Teachers must do all that they can to make sure that they are really communicating to parents in the reports that they write. All too often, especially in the upper primary and secondary schools, reports list a series of marks, perhaps as percentages or as symbols (A, B, C, D, E,), give an indication as to how these compare with those obtained by other children in the class and conclude with a few words such as, 'good work', 'has made progress', and the very common 'could do better'. Such reports tell most parents very little, and, unless there are real and frequent opportunities for them to talk to their children's teacher, are not enough. Although it is time consuming and not always easy to write additional paragraphs about every child so as to help their parents to understand them and their needs, it is time and effort well spent, especially if the emphasis is not so much on blaming the child for any shortcomings but rather on what he has achieved and what more can be done at home to help him. A paragraph such as the following is informative and personal to the parents.

> Sipiwe is still finding reading difficult but has worked very hard at it this term and is now able to read short and simple stories for enjoyment, especially if she is given encouragement. The progress she has made will increase if you can find the time to sit with her for a few minutes every day while she reads to you from the books which I am sending home with her, and to talk to her about what she has read. I should welcome a discussion with you at a time convenient to us both.

We all appreciate being treated as though we are important and have something to offer and a teacher who ignores this need in parents is doing a disservice to both parents and pupils.

Application 19

1   In a school of the age range in which you expect to teach, make a summary of the most commonly used assessment procedures. How clearly do they measure the aspects of educational progress which they are intended to measure? While not appearing to the school and its staff to be critical of its procedures, what alterations, if any, would you like to propose, and why? If they seem satisfactory as they are to you, also say why.
Discuss your experience and proposals with a small group of fellow students.

2   Try to remember the assessment, including examination, procedures which were used in the school at which you were a pupil. How accurate, comprehensive and constructive did they seem to be and how would you have wished them to be modified?

Application 20

In an educational district accessible to you, find out what facilities exist for more specialist assessment and remedial assistance than can normally be undertaken by a class teacher. How adequately do they seem to cover the need?

Further reading

Again, there are several general texts commonly on college library shelves which will fill out this topic for you.
Some examples are:
Child, Dennis, *Psychology and the Teacher*, (Third edition), London, Holt Rinehart and Winston, 1980, Chapters 13 and 14 (from page 284).
Vander Zanden (ibid) Chapter 18, p. 462.

CHAPTER THIRTEEN

Guidance and counselling: the role of the teacher and the school

It has been stressed throughout this book that the teacher's and the school's responsibility is not merely to ensure that the pupils acquire the academic skills and knowledge which the curriculum and syllabuses propose. They also have the responsibility of ensuring that each pupil matures steadily along his own personal line. This means that they are responsible for planning the learning experiences, activities, attitudes and relationships so that as many as possible of each pupil's basic psychological needs are satisfied through the medium of his education.

In this sense the whole curriculum and everything that teachers do within it have a guidance function, in that they play an important role in determining the direction that each pupil's development will take.

In addition to the general guidance offered by the total education process, each teacher, however, must be ready to accept a more direct and personal role as both guide and counsellor, using the term *guidance* to cover the activities designed to direct and promote developmental progress in a general way and *counselling* to cover activities which offer more personal help to individuals and their parents. There are several aspects of a teacher's guidance and counselling roles which are worth itemising, so as to focus attention on some that he might have overlooked.

1 He is, as has just been mentioned, a planner and manager of educational experiences for his pupils, which will contribute to the development of the knowledge, skills, personal qualities, habits of thought and decision making and attitudes to themselves and to others which is a preparation for adulthood.

2   He is in the position of being a trusted confidante to all his pupils, not by invading their privacy but by his attitude towards them, showing that he is ready to listen and help whenever they need him.

3   He is someone in a unique position to monitor the development and progress of all his pupils and thus he may be the first to be aware of individuals who are showing early signs of developmental and behavioural problems. Early awareness, more than anything else, can prevent serious difficulties from arising later.

4   Because of his facilities for giving early help he is in the best position to decide when additional help may be needed with a problem individual, for diagnosis and treatment.

5   Finally, he is a communication centre, with links not only with the children but also with their parents and other teachers.

It can be seen, then, that the general guidance role can merge into that of counsellor, the teacher's responsibility being what is often called one of *pastoral care*. This means that his concern is with the whole human being who brings with him into the classroom all the experiences of his out of school life.

Although all teachers of children at all ages have the guidance and counselling responsibility, the circumstances and emphases may vary at different levels. In the early school years, their main concern is likely to be with difficulties of social and emotional adjustment to school and to other children which some of their pupils may have. After the initial anxiety that most children feel at going to school for the first time, most settle down happily. Some, however, find it more difficult and the teacher must be on the lookout, not only for the shy, fearful and lonely individual but also for the one who shows his lack of social skill by bullying and aggressive behaviour. The teacher's role is both that of guide and counsellor, by arranging the class activities so that everyone is involved and has a chance to practise good group and co-operative behaviour, and by quietly drawing the reluctant ones in while restraining the aggressors. At this age children are fairly easily influenced by group pressures and expectations and, if given the opportunity, are usually willing to co-operate with the teacher in helping the lonely and the frightened. Some extra attention by the teacher which shows that he understands the child's worries and is able to give support and confidence usually improves matters considerably. Equally, the disruptive, aggressive, bullying and uncooperative individual can often be helped to readjust with some personal attention from the teacher, whose natural annoyance with such behaviour should not be allowed to lead to confrontation and punishment in the usual sense. In most cases, children showing these behaviours need as much reassurance about their ability and worthiness as do the frightened ones. They, too, need to be shown that, while their aggressive behaviour does not achieve the results that they hope it will, they can nevertheless be useful members of the group, especially if they can be given a special responsibility within their capacity.

Very occasionally there may be a child so remote and withdrawn or so aggressive and disruptive, that the teacher's efforts seem to make very little headway. In such cases the teacher would be wise to talk to the parents as soon as possible, usually after consultation with the school Head. There are many family circumstances that can reinforce adjustment problems, including relationships with relatives, and their attitudes towards the child. It is important that the teacher should not himself probe these circumstances directly, partly because he does not have the expertise to do so and partly because direct probing is rarely successful and can be very misleading. His role should rather be to express his concern that, despite all his efforts he has not been able to make much progress in improving the social, and consequently the educational, adjustment of the child. He should aim at making clear to the parents his causes for concern about the child and ask for their suggestions and co-operation, being careful not to give the impression that he wants them to punish or penalise the child, (measures that are likely to make matters worse), but to reinforce his own efforts. A word of warning is necessary at this point, which applies to all teachers of all ages of pupil, and that is that they must be careful not state firm conclusions about the causes of problems on flimsy evidence. Amateur 'psychologising' of this sort can sometimes be misleading, if not impertinent. If, after all his efforts and those of co-operating children and parents, there is no real improvement and the child is genuinely being handicapped in his progress and development, it should be suggested that professional help be sought from whatever psychological services are available. On rare occasions, extreme emotional and behavioural maladjustment can be a symptom of a more serious mental health problem.

As the child progresses through the upper primary school, situations in which guidance and counselling skills are called on do not change much. The emphasis is still on providing learning activities and social situations which are suitable for the children and providing guidance for their behaviour, while remaining watchful for individuals who may not be adjusting and progressing as they should. In this period, learning difficulties too extreme to be managed in the normal classroom may become apparent, though such a conclusion should be drawn only after possible physical handicaps such as defective sight and hearing have been ruled out. Because most children in this period are content to conform and co-operate provided their educational arrangements are suitable to their age and needs, the individual who is widely deviant from the rest probably needs some action to be taken. The commonest symptoms at this time, though it must be stressed they are still rare, include extreme isolation of an individual from the rest of the group and the teacher. Such a child sometimes seems to be overwhelmingly sad and joyless, even though he may achieve well enough in the classroom. Because of his reasonable level of attainment he may be overlooked in a busy classroom, but such a person, especially if the condition is more than a brief passing mood and does not respond to the teacher's efforts, is urgently in need of professional help, and the school authorities and parents should be consulted.

A greater nuisance to the teacher and the class is the individual who continually interrupts, disrupts the activities, and is restless, aggressive and argumentative without applying himself to his work. Often, there are outbursts of real anger on apparently little provocation which can cause him to be a threat to his own and other's safety. Here again it is more then mere 'naughtiness' and lack of discipline. Sometimes a great deal of persistence by a teacher who tries to avoid situations which cause tension can help, but if the situation continues to the detriment of the class and the teacher, help must be sought. Sometimes medical treatment can alleviate the problem.

In a different category is the irregular attender who is suspected of playing truant or inventing minor illnesses to avoid going to school. There are many possible causes for this, and obviously the first thing to do is to check for hidden bullying by other children, or to find out whether he has lost confidence in his teacher or someone else in the school. Often it is a symptom of a deeper anxiety which consultation with and co-operation by parents might help. If this fails professional help should be sought.

Once the child has moved into the secondary school the teacher's and the school's guidance and counselling roles become wider. For most adolescents, important decisions and choices have to be made about their futures during this period, and a great deal hinges not merely on their level of academic attainment but also on their readiness for making these decisions and choices. The school and the teacher have an important part to play in helping young people to make the most sensible choices. Guidance comes into play mainly in the opportunities that the curriculum itself and the school programme offer for adolescents to learn some of the skills which they will need to run their adult lives successfully. For example, they need to know something about what working for their living means, how to find and apply for work and the qualities sought by employers such as integrity, punctuality, honesty, loyalty, etc.. In order to be able to decide on the sort of work they will seek they need to know not only what sorts of jobs exist but also what each one entails, the sort of skills and qualifications needed, the demands it makes on the worker and the nature of the work itself and the lifestyle likely to develop from it. Preparation for vocational choice in the wider sense is a matter, at first, for group and class guidance and should form part of the basic curriculum of the school, such as a regular programme of visits, discussions, films, talks by professionals etc., which at least the pupils in their final year should attend. Group guidance as part of the curriculum should also include such financial matters as budgeting, hire purchase, credit buying and insurance. The maintenance of personal health through good dietary habits should also feature in the guidance programme. Other areas which are often overlooked in the curriculum are the civic responsibilities of all individuals, and preparation for responsible sexual behaviour and ultimate parenthood. Carefully planned programmes in which the young people have a chance to develop a basis upon which they can make well informed choices both before and after they have left school, should be an integral part of every secondary school timetable, or that of the upper primary school for those who do not have a chance of secondary schooling.

Fears, sometimes expressed by teachers, that the 'serious' purpose of secondary education. i.e. academic study, will be put at risk by the invasion of non-examinable programmes, are groundless. Indeed, it has been shown that pupils who are included in lively, interesting guidance programmes (though not necessarily under that name) are more likely to make an effort in the more traditional school subjects too. One of the more serious problems which quite often affects secondary school pupils, is that of disillusionment and boredom, and a feeling that what they are being expected to learn is not relevant to their immediate interests.

Such a feeling is not always confined to the less successful learner and the resultant lowered motivation can have longterm harmful effects. At this point, it is necessary to say that the attitude of the teacher who is planning and presenting the guidance programmes outlined above can be an important factor in their success or failure. A teacher who is reluctant and not convinced that such programmes are of value inevitably conveys this feeling to his class, many of whom will begin to agree with him. In Zimbabwe, an imaginative course called 'Education for Living' was introduced into the timetable for school leavers' classes and the initial results showed clearly the influence of the teachers and the school heads, and the need, first of all, to convince them of its purpose and importance. At least at first, some parents and pupils also needed convincing, especially those who were heavily committed to obtaining good results in their school leaving examinations. Some thought that it was a useful addition to the curriculum for the less academic but not for the rest, with predictable results.

The teacher's counselling role also becomes more important during the secondary school period. For example, especially in the higher forms, there are often subject and course choices within the school which have to be made by and for the pupils. There is considerable variation between countries and districts, and even schools, but where there are choices available, the teacher has the responsibility of ensuring that decisions are made in the best interests of each individual, which implies that he must himself have a detailed knowledge of the educational and vocational effects of selecting or rejecting the available course options. In addition, he should have available as much information as possible (preferably in the form of a detailed cumulative record such as was described in the previous chapter) so that he can advise whether the demands of the options being considered are suitable for the particular individual's abilities and needs. A major aim should be make sure that no pupil is allowed to close off educational or employment avenues that he may later want to follow.

His counselling role may also extend to giving help to individual pupils and their parents about vocational choices. Ideally, vocational counselling is a specialist matter and requires the counsellor to have an extensive knowledge of the likely availability of different jobs, the formal qualifications needed and the actual demands of the job itself, so that the young person can make better choices to suit his interests and abilities.

Specialist vocational counsellors sometimes use standardised tests of abilities and interests to help in selection but the results of these should be used cautiously, perhaps as a basis for discussing further ideas rather than as a firm pointer to a career choice which should be made. The vocational counsellor should be knowledgeable about possible jobs or courses, and about the individual concerned. He should also develop important skills and attitudes. For example, his job is not to decide *for* the individual, telling him firmly what he should or should not do. Rather, he should aim at giving the necessary information and then at widening the individual's thinking about what he *could* do. The actual decision must genuinely be that of the pupil and his parents, and not that of the teacher, even though some pupils and parents think that they would like to have the decision made for them. To summarise, any non-specialist, given the specific task of vocational or careers' counselling in a school, should at least read further and investigate locally. The better he knows his pupils and the alternative choices, the more likely he is to be able to help. This is especially true in developing countries where professional counselling facilities may still be rudimentary and career possibilities unclear.

Adolescence is a time when not only is the individual becoming sexually mature, with the tensions and decisions that that can entail, but he is also conscious of moving towards post-school decision making and early adulthood. There are greater opportunities for situations of some conflict arising, both when trying to balance immediate wants with the demands of longer term goals and when trying to reconcile their own changing expectations and increasing desire for independence with those of their parents, their peers and their school.

The problem may be particularly acute in countries where the adolescent has come from a traditional, often rural home, into a school which has opened his mind to many other ideas than those available to his parents and extended family. As the time to end his schooling comes he may feel reluctant to return to the life that his culture would expect of him. Or he may already be involved in traditional activities leading to his acceptance into the full adult life of his community. This may make him impatient with the apparently lesser status that his school gives him. Alternatively he may abuse the different freedoms which he has at school compared with those of his home to behave in ways disapproved of by both home and school. Adolescent girls from traditional backgrounds may have even more apparent cause for discontent when contemplating returning to their homes as young adults. In addition they are often subject to sexual pressures from boys at school from which their home environments protect them.

Contrary to some popular opinion, most adolescents adjust competently and progress happily towards adulthood. However, there is a period when a few, most often those whose earlier experiences did not always fulfill their psychological needs at the time, are unable to manage the additional demands of this period of development and cause concern to their parents and teachers. In such cases teachers have an important role to play, especially if they have been able to build up their pupils' confidence in them and to come to know them well enough to be able to recognise those few individuals who need help.

The first warning sign which should alert a teacher is a very noticeable and prolonged deterioration is an individual's behaviour, attainment and attitude to his work. Everyone, child as well as adult, has short periods when things do not seem to go smoothly and teachers must be careful not to exaggerate their importance. An unobtrusive and watchful eye is usually all that is necessary and the situation rights itself. But when the changed behaviour becomes progressively more marked he should take some action. A quiet, friendly, unemotional talk with the individual in which the teacher tells the pupil that he is worried about him and his school progress, and would like to help, is sometimes enough. Quiet enquiries among colleagues may reveal some special problem and an early opportunity should be sought to talk to the parents, care being taken not to give the impression that complaints are being made about the individual but rather to express concern and a desire to help. The fact that someone shows concern rather than blame and offers comfortably relaxed opportunities for discussion of problems is often enough, especially if accompanied by support for constructively-changed attitudes and expectations from others where possible.

A relatively recent reaction by a few distressed adolescents is to start taking one of the mood-changing drugs, ranging from alcohol to the so-called 'soft' drugs of marijuana (Indian Hemp), sometimes known as 'pot', the more dangerous glue-sniffing, cocaine or LSD. Unfortunately these and similar drugs are becoming increasingly available in developing countries and adolescents are very vulnerable to persuasive dealers. It is probable that, because of a well developed sense of curiosity and a desire for experience, many young people try a soft drug at least once, most of them never to repeat the experience. Those who move positively into the so-called 'drug-culture' are most likely to be those whose social and emotional psychological needs are not adequately satisfied and they seek status and recognition among groups whose purpose is obtaining and using drugs. The fact that such drugs give a feeling of greater power and self-assurance, or reduce uncomfortable tensions, thus giving a false feeling of contentment, is often the initial reason for becoming more than briefly involved with them. Unfortunately, the more one relies on drugs to solve problems the more problems one has, and the need for drugs continues, the individual becoming psychologically dependent on them. Some, too, may cause physiological dependence, which means that the body's tissues grow to need the chemical substance of the drug to function apparently normally. There can be a further complication in that the supply of drugs becomes increasingly expensive so that the addict resorts to crime to obtain money to pay for them, or to settle debts to the drug sellers who are unscrupulous in their demands for payment.

While teachers should be careful not to assume that every problem adolescent is involved with drugs, it is a possibility that should not be overlooked. The chief symptoms, in addition to a significant alteration in attainment and social participation, include unusual changes of mood with swings between inactivity and excitement, and an increasing secretiveness and withdrawal from the main stream of school activity. Some drugs, such as marijuana, have a distinctive smell which can linger on clothes and breath. The immediate effects of excessive alcohol are commonly known and should be considered by teachers as potentially as dangerous as the other 'soft' drugs. If a teacher suspects drug involvement he must be very careful how he approaches the problem. It is important to remember that in many countries the possession and use of certain drugs, including alcohol, is illegal and once the civil authorities are involved the consequences are more than the particular individual needs in order to reform. So, before involving the authorities in further investigation, the teacher must be sure that his diagnosis is very likely to be correct. Quiet, unobtrusive attempts should be made to talk to the individual, not necessarily asking him outright whether he is taking drugs but rather expressing concern at his apparent anxiety and unhappiness and offering to help. At an early stage, the Head of the school and the parents should be consulted and the possibility of drug abuse discussed. Sometimes the expression of concern and the renewal of the individual's confidence in parents and teachers, combined with the knowledge of the possible medical and legal consequences of illicit drug taking will persuade him to turn away from them. But there could come a time when for an individual's own good the professional services will be needed, though one hopes that the recommendation is for cure rather than punishment.

As with every other aspect of human development, prevention is better than cure and the education system has the responsibility of making sure that no one is ignorant of the effects of habitual drugabuse. While knowledge of the physiological and legal results of such abuse are unlikely in themselves to stop young people turning to drugs in misguided attempt to fulfil their psychological needs, the merely curious are more likely to avoid experimentation. It is a well proven fact that human beings will put themselves in danger even when they are aware of the possible consequences, if, thereby, they will satisfy other strong needs. For example, the author investigated the relationship between the extent of factual knowledge that secondary school boys had about Bilharzia (schistosomiasis) and the incidence of the disease among them.

Bilharzia is a water-borne parasitic disease endemic in Africa and elsewhere in the world. The parasite enters the body through the pores of the skin during contact with infected water and its eggs accumulate in many of the body's organs and cause extensive damage leading at best to lethargy and at worst to serious illness and even death. The investigation was among a group of the population which, for geographical and economic reasons, could easily avoid contact with rivers and other areas of contaminated water. All the boys, at intervals throughout their school careers, had lessons on the causes, effects, prevention and treatment of the disease and in the study almost every boy demonstrated that he had a very detailed knowledge of the complex life-cycle of the parasite, how it infects the body and its effects. Nevertheless, a very high proportion of the boys had been relatively recently infected by the parasite and it soon became obvious that they were more afraid of being thought cowardly by their peers when they avoided infection than they were of the disease. The relative lack of success of anti-smoking campaigns among the young and vulnerable is further illustration that knowledge by itself does not protect everyone, the best protection being a secure, satisfying home, school and social environment which allows the essential human needs to be satisfied. On the other hand, factual knowledge offered in a non dramatic and thus believable way, will give a sound basis for personal decision making about drugs, smoking and other potentially harmful habits for very many young people. The school and the teacher both have vital roles to play through the pastoral care that they offer.

Application 21

1 In a school at the level at which you are most likely to teach, discuss and describe:
   a) the extent to which the curriculum and the teacher's interpretation of it fulfill the school's guidance role;
   b) the commonest situations in which the teacher is called on to fulfill the pastoral care and counselling roles.
   If you were a member of the school staff what would you do to fulfill these functions?
2 What other guidance and counselling facilities are available in the school to give support to teacher (the Head? specially designated staff members? etc.) and what are available in the educational system when more specialist help is needed?

If possible work with another student and/or discuss your findings and ideas with him and with other fellow students.

Further reading

You should find out more about what is relevant to your own circumstances from local colleges and universities. A thorough reading of Thompson (ibid), especially Part IV, will give you some principles from which you can develop your own approaches.

CHAPTER FOURTEEN

Psychology and the curriculum

The emphasis so far in this book has been on *who* is being educated, *where* and *why* they are being educated and *how* this may be achieved. It has considered the nature, abilities and developmental processes of the learners and how to make use of this knowledge to ensure that the intended learning takes place. It is time now to focus more closely on the content of education, that is on the curriculum.

First of all, we must be clear about what is meant by the word *curriculum*, but before we discuss this you should undertake the following task so that you will know something about the commonly held ideas about the school curriculum and how some teachers see their role in relation to it.

Application 22

1   Ask the following questions of:
    a) a Head of a school,
    b) a teacher with considerable experience,
    c) a teacher with less than five years teaching experience,
    who are working in the level of school in which you eventually hope to teach (infants, lower primary, upper primary, secondary, etc.).
    Note the answers so that you can look at them later in the light of the discussion that follows.

    Questions
    (i) What do you think is included in the term 'school curriculum'?
    (ii) (for Heads) How much control over the school curriculum do you have?
    (iii) (for class teachers) How much control over the class or subject curriculum do you have?
    (iv) Who do you think is responsible in the end for deciding what the curriculum should be?

189

2   Think back to your own school days, if possible sharing ideas with fellow students. What do you now think were the main features of the curriculum which you experienced?
Discuss this under the following headings:
(i) aims and objectives of that curriculum;
(ii) who made the main decisions about the curriculum;
(iii) how far individual teachers seemed to be able to make curriculum decisions.

You may have found that the emphasis in the answers that you have had to your questions and, indeed in your perception of your own school curriculum, was on the syllabuses which were followed in the class lessons and the examinations results which seemed to be the major purpose of the curriculum. This emphasis is especially likely in newly expanding and developing education systems, for historical reasons. In the past, the opportunities for schooling were often very limited, particularly at the post-primary levels. At the same time, professional, economic and social advancement very much depended on educational qualifications, which could best be shown by the possession of a recognised certificate or diploma which recorded examination successes in a range of subjects. In many instances, the subjects studied for examination purposes, their syllabuses and the ultimate examination questions were decided on, administered and marked by people in Northern Hemisphere countries far away from those for whom they were intended. When one looks at the tiny proportion of children who began their education at the bottom of the primary school and who managed to reach the top and successfully pass the final examinations, one can understand that the main purpose of education and thus its curriculum, tended to be the covering of pre-set subject syllabuses in such a way that the pupils would pass the examinations.

Often, the process of educational selection began at the lowest levels of the primary school, only those who made sufficient progress in learning the accepted skills and knowledge being allowed to go on to the next class. Most of the rest were not re-admitted to the school, only a minority being allowed to repeat the previous year's work in the hope that they would 'catch up'. Human and financial resources were so limited that the provision for individual differences in ability, age and home background were very scarce. The picture was commonly of very large classes and very little equipment and material. All that even the most dedicated teachers could do was to offer their pupils identical experiences in the hope that at least the potentially most able would learn enough to continue their schooling.

It is also important to remember that the majority of experienced teachers, as well as the professionals and administrators in the newly independent Third World countries, themselves came through such a system. They represent the successful ones, those who managed to jump all the educational hurdles put in their way, or who had sufficient sound educational grounding to be able to undertake further study by correspondence, or in other countries. There is an all too human tendency for people to accept that the system in which they were successful is a good system. They often want their own children to have the same experience. In such countries it is even more vital that not only those with authority and influence but also the least experienced teacher should look at and think about the school curriculum, both in its broad aim and in its classroom detail.

In the past, then, the school curriculum tended to be seen by teachers solely as the content of the laid-down syllabuses, their task being to ensure that as many of their pupils as possible are able to demonstrate that they have developed the required skills (reading, writing, etc.) and learned the facts and ideas that are included in them. While the content of the syllabuses is an important aspect of the school curriculum, teachers need to have a wider knowledge of what the purposes of the school are so that they can plan for their pupils to have the sort of learning experiences which will not only ensure that they learn what is intended but also that they will develop the personal and social qualities that they will need in their own world. It is particularly important in newly-developing education systems that the school curricula be developed to suit their pupils' and their country's real needs, which are likely to be different in emphasis from those in older, industrialised countries.

It may seem at this stage of your training and experience, that you can have very little influence on such important and wide-ranging matters. Indeed it is very likely that a great deal of high level planning is currently taking place to establish curricula for systems in your own country, and you will, rightly, be expected to work within the guidelines established. Nevertheless, the more you are aware of the processes of curriculum development, their psychological implications and the purposes that they are intended to achieve, the better teacher you will become. As has been said before in this book, learning is more successful if the learner knows why it is needed, where it fits into the overall topic and what he should be able to do as a result of that learning. The same principle applies to the work of a teacher.

The full meaning of the word curriculum, then, must include *everything* that the schools *plans* for, or *intends*, its pupils to do and experience: the range of subjects formally on the timetable, the scope of each subject, the ways in which progress is assessed, the social structure of the school and the opportunities that it offers to work in groups of teams and to work independently and accept responsibility for oneself and others. Also included, are the cultural and leisure activities available, the extent to which they 'learn how to learn' and to think independently and logically, as well as to identify with and feel part of the community. Such a wide definition of the school curriculum means that not only the officials who are responsible for curriculum development but also the Heads of schools, and the teachers themselves must be clear what the results of the education that they offer should be for their pupils. This applies not only to the formal knowledge and skills that they possess but also to the personal and social qualities and attitudes that they develop. This latter aspect is often known as the 'hidden curriculum' because it does not appear on the formal syllabuses and in discussed more fully on page 202. It is important that those involved in education think of the curriculum not as something fixed and determined entirely by someone else but as a continually changing process within the limits imposed by the needs and capacities of each pupil and those of the community within which he lives and which provides the education.

The foregoing is not an easy concept, especially for the inexperienced teacher. It will clarify things if one thinks of the curriculum first of all in general terms, as shown in the diagram opposite. On the outside is the community, which is not just the local neighbourhood but a geographical or administrative region, or even a whole country, and includes all the individuals and groups among whom the pupils now live and where they are most likely to take their place as citizens. The main, general purpose of education systems is to prepare the young for their adulthood, supplementing their families' and neighbourhood's efforts. To achieve this purpose and to justify the money and effort that the community puts into it, the overall curriculum adopted by the school system must be planned with the real needs of the wider community in mind. It must do its best to ensure that the pupils who will eventually emerge at the end of their education are not merely literate but that it will be possible for the community to find among them enough people with the knowledge, ability and readiness to develop the special skills that it will need, both

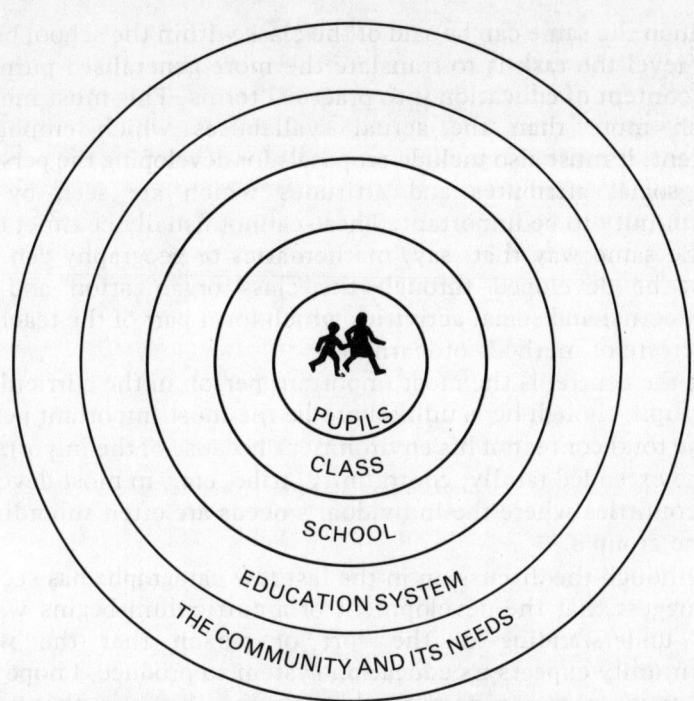

technical and professional. It must ensure as far as possible that it produces young people who will be able to live as healthy and responsible adult members of their community, both within its economy and within its social, political and domestic life. Since each community requires different things of its members, in differing proportions, it follows that to achieve its purpose, the overall educational curriculum must be planned in the light of a realistic assessment of the country's or community's needs.

Moving to the next circle in the diagram we find the school embedded within the educational system. The school curriculum has the overall purpose of contributing to the achievement of the whole educational system. Those responsible for its planning must have a clear idea of the particular contribution that it should make, the emphasis and details being different for different age groups and ability levels. Each successive school level must build on what has gone on at previous levels, while leading clearly to the next one. A school curriculum developed in isolation from, or in ignorance of, the needs of the pupil within his community and his present levels of knowledge and skill, is unlikely to be successful.

Much the same can be said of the class within the school but at this level the task is to translate the more generalised purposes and content of education into practical terms. This must include much more than the actual syallabuses which emphasise content; it must also include proposals for developing the personal and social attributes and attitudes which are seen by the community to be important. These cannot usually be timetabled in the same way that, say, mathematics or geography can, but must be developed through the class organization and the intellectual and social activities which form part of the teacher's repertoire of methods of learning.

At the centre, is the most important person in the curriculum, the pupil, though he is unlikely to be the most important person in the total context of his environment because of the importance of the extended family, community, tribe, etc., in most developing countries where the individual's needs are often subordinate to the group's.

Although the discussion in the last few paragraphs has seemed to suggest that the development of a curriculum begins with a real understanding of the sort of person that the wider community expects its education system to produce, I hope that the major message coming through this book is that to be successful, any educational experience must fit the immediate needs and abilities of the individual learner. Thus, it is important that those people who are involved at any level in educational curricula have a practical understanding of the psychology of development and learning as well as of the wider purpose of education. The class teacher, who is at the front line in the process, has the most important and often difficult job of ensuring that his own efforts fit in with the overall curriculum. But he must remember that, in a sense, each pupil is following his own individual curriculum, in that each one has needs different from everyone else's. Fortunately there is enough common ground of content and development to make the teacher's task possible.

The Curriculum in developing education systems

You have probably realised that the first consideration of any curriculum is its objectives, i.e. what it is intended to achieve. We have already seen how important it is to identify objectives and how to achieve them in classroom learning.

Curriculum objectives

Curriculum objectives can be looked for under the following headings.

1 (a) The fields of knowledge that are important for everyone to have in order to be a happy and useful citizen, though, in the nature of things, not everyone will be able to attain the same level of competence.

(b) The fields of special knowledge which the country needs to ensure that it can be efficient economically, industrially and administratively.

2 The intellectual skills and habits which the community would like its members to have, so that they can make responsible decisions about their own lives and as members of the wider community.

3 The personal qualities, such as integrity, loyalty, co-operativeness, independence of thought and action, willingness to accept responsibility for self and others, and so on, which may be valued by the community. Under this heading also comes behaviour and attitudes, such as those which affect relationships with other people, parents, children, the aged and handicapped, those in authority, minority and other groups within the community, and so on.

You will see from this list that in developing a curriculum for any system, a great deal more than the syllabus content must be considered. Much of the foregoing, while not being developed only by the school but by the child's experience in his home and his own social group, forms an important part of the school programme and must be planned for within the school and class organization and the learning teaching methods adopted by the teacher.

No attempt will be made in this book to prescribe what should be included in any particular curriculum, because every system has different purposes. There are some important principles to be considered and questions to be asked, which may act as a guide.

Fields of knowledge

Language and literacy

One of the first decisions that has to be made in any developing education system is about the language in which the children are to be taught, and how and when to introduce it if it is different from the home language. In some Third World countries which were formerly administered by a major Western power, education was through the medium of a language such as English or French, and success in examinations heavily dependent on competence in that language. Because many developing education systems are in countries where there is a wide range of vernacular languages and dialects, a major objective is to develop competence in the 'foreign' language, both because it can help to unify the peoples of the country by providing them with a common tongue, and to ensure that it is possible to communicate and co-operate with other countries. For example, in the international organizations in Africa, such as the OAU or the SADCC countries, where mutual understanding is important, French, English and sometimes Arabic are used, languages which are widespread throughout the regions.

If a major objective of the education system is to ensure literacy in a language other than the learner's own home one, consideration must be given in the curriculum to the best age at which to introduce it and how this can best be done. It is here that educational psychology may be able to help. Experience suggests that children should have their first schooling through the medium of their home language and learn their basic reading skills in it. As has been said before, learning must be based on the familiar and gradually be extended outwards to new realms. Experiments have been carried out to see how far children are able to learn, for example in English, right from the beginning of their schooling. The results showed that while the more able pupils, especially those who were already at least partly familiar with the language, made good progress, the less able pupils tended to become very confused, the seeds of educational failure being sown early in their lives. On the other hand, where the second language has been introduced for the first time at the secondary level, especially if it was confined to set periods on the timetable and learned in some isolation from the rest of the curriculum, the likelihood of real fluency was considerably reduced. The most successful way to help learners to become truly bi-lingual (i.e. able to use two languages fluently) is to introduce words and phrases in the second language gradually into all aspects of the timetable fairly soon after the pupils have settled into the school, at first only as a matter of interest. The injection of new words, phrases and sentences should be introduced gradually, always ensuring that the new ideas are understood through the home language as well as through the second one, until the balance of presentation and learning, after several years, moves from the home to the second language. Any language is learned most successfully if used as much as possible in everyday ways; only much later might it be useful to analyse some of the grammatical construction, and only then if the rules identified are used to improve understanding and accuracy of usage.

A further important consideration when planning for education through two languages is the status of the home language, which is an important part of an individual's culture. If the impression is given to the learner that his home tongue is inferior to that of the more widely used one, it may have long term consequences, perhaps giving some speakers of a minority language feelings of inferiority, or leading to separation from their background and personal history, or even cause them to look down on those members of their families who are not bi-lingual.

Another difficulty still being encountered by some developing education systems is that of suitable reading matter, both in the vernacular and the second language, available books often having been written by people who do not have enough first hand knowledge either of the pupils' personal experiences and interests, or of the level and complexity of ideas with which they can deal. Curriculum planning, both by the professional and the class teacher, must take these difficulties into consideration. The latter might consider writing some of his own books, especially for the younger learners, based on his knowledge of their interests, abilities and educational needs.

Mathematics, science and technical education

Every community also needs its members to be able to understand the purposes and processes of mathematics in such a way that they can use them in everyday life, in simple calculations, measuring quantities, handling money satisfactorily, and planning those many aspects of their lives which involve numbers. Curricula in mathematics education usually have the same objectives in all education systems; the difference lies in the sorts of things that the learner will have to be able to do with their knowledge and the sorts of situations in which they will need to use it. For example, children in an African village could learn arithmetic through problems related to the land, the crops, rainfall and its distribution, the length of time seeds take to germinate and how much seed and fertilizer is needed for certain sized tracts of land. They also need to be able to calculate the cost of food and other items which have to be bought, and the budgeting of available money. The emphasis for urban pupils may be different, though they must learn the same mathematical processes as their rural cousins. The teacher has the task of identifying the mathematical needs of the pupils he teaches, using materials and examples that are real to the learners and which are likely to be ones that they will themselves use. Most Third World countries have a less-technical tradition than do the more industrialised ones, so that there is a need to make a special effort to ensure a sound basic mathematical understanding among the young, since mathematics is a foundation for technical knowledge. Not all pupils by any means will become technicians but without an effective mathematical curriculum it may not be possible to find enough young people to become the technicians that the country needs.

While on the subject of the urgent need felt in Third World countries for people with technical expertise to ensure that they can make the most of their resources and improve the physical quality of their people's lives, it is important that from the earliest school years there should be a scientific component in the curriculum. By this it is not meant that formal and theoretical science or physics lessons should be taught throughout the school programme; rather, the children's natural curiosity about the world around them, how things work, why things behave in a certain way, what would happen if we did this, should be stimulated wherever possible. There is evidence to suggest that the traditional explanations of some natural events may hamper true observation. Throughout history, among all people, mythical and mystical explanations have existed until eventually it becomes the custom and educational tradition to question them and to seek explanations which fit the real facts. For example, if one believes that crop failure is the result of the influence of a bad spirit, the birth of twins the result of infidelity, or that hyenas turn into witches and make people ill, one is likely to use inappropriate ways to deal with the events. The best way to counteract the effect of similar widely held but unscientific beliefs is to include in the curriculum a wide range of activities suitable to the pupils' ages and interests, which will gradually develop in them an understanding of the rules which govern the physical world. Even small children can grow seeds in different sorts or soil, with different amounts of watering, and observe the variation in growth. They can be encouraged to observe and ask questions... where does the rain come from? what is thunder?

what makes us ill? Later they can construct simple models to learn, for example, how to reduce soil erosion, to preserve food by sterilisation and excluding flies from it, etc.. Clues as to what technical matters are important for them to learn about must come from the homes and the locality. Urban children may be ready for more sophisticated ideas, such as piped water, drainage, electricity, the internal combustion engine, etc., at an earlier age than may rural pupils. Children from more industrialised countries have many more opportunities for learning about their technical world than do most children from less industrialised ones, yet the world in which the latter are growing will be more technically oriented than is their present one and they need to be prepared, not only to understand it but to make a contribution to its development through the work which many will later undertake.

Personal health and hygiene are also areas which Third World countries, even more than older ones, need to include in the school curriculum. Although a great deal of progress is being made in most newer countries in expanding medical services and primary health care, the existing resources are usually over-stretched, never quite catching up because of the speed at which most populations are increasing. The education system must accept some responsibility for ensuring that its pupils develop an understanding of their own bodies and how they work, diet, cleanliness and the avoidance of preventible diseases. In this way, not only will the children be healthier and thus happier in themselves, but they will be better able to teach their own children such things later on.

Cultural subjects
There is much more knowledge that children need from their school curriculum. Everyone, for example, needs to know and appreciate something about his own origins, his own people's history, geography, literature, music and art. In the fairly recent past there was a tendency to select syallabuses which were about the history, geography and culture of other countries, especially at the later examination level. Often the cultural subjects which were offered, such as music, drama, art and indigenous literature, were minimal because they were not themselves formally examined for certification purposes. Part of the problem, too, was that local material was not always easily available to teachers, a situation still partly found in some places today. But teachers and pupils can themselves develop and collect their own materials to

supplement the existing ones, at the same time learning about themselves and other people and developing a respect for the past and their apparently less sophisticated ancestors which might otherwise be overlooked, widening the 'generation gap' mentioned earlier.

Here, then, are just some of the considerations when deciding on the fields of knowledge that should be included in the education system's overall currciulum. As can be seen, a great deal is required of the teacher, especially in identifying the real needs of his pupils in their community and within the wider society in which they will live. A well planned and taught curriculum will in itself add to the progress which the community will make as those who have experienced it become adults.

Intellectual skills and habits

When planning the educational provision for life in a particular society it is important for the planners to decide what mental processes it needs its members to develop. As was seen earlier in this book, within individual limits the ways in which the mind works, tackles problems and makes decisions can be influenced by educational and other experiences. For example, an authoritarian system in which pupils have to learn the same things in the same way, accepting without question the authority of the teacher or the textbook, is likely to produce a high proportion of people who tend to accept authority without question in their daily lives. On the other hand, a system which encourages its members to question, to analyse, to compare, to experiment for themselves and thus have confidence in their own decisions, is likely to produce people who continue to use their minds in this way, as adults. A system which enables its members to learn how to learn is likely to produce people who will retain their curiosity into adult life, which in itself helps them to continue to improve their ability to think clearly and sensibly.

It is very unlikely that any country, developing or otherwise, would deny that it expects its educational provision to produce not only knowledgeable people, but people who can continue to learn, reason, make independent judgements based on facts, can resist appeals to superstition and prejudice and so on. All too often, however, this aspect of the school curriculum is taken for granted and is not sufficiently emphasised. The desired intellectual skills cannot be taught by themselves but must be in the front of teachers' minds when they are planning how their pupils will learn the content matter of the syllabuses. Fortunately, the most successful learning methods are those which expect the learner to ask questions, look for answers, experiment for himself explain to others and find logical patterns. The sort of testing and examination procedures, too, can govern the sort of mental activities demanded of the learner and must be included in the curriculum planning process.

Third World countries are likely to need to pay particular attention to the sorts of intellectual abilities which should be developed. Historically, much formal education was directed at fact collection and examination passing, which often seemed to prevent the use of the sorts of learning methods mentioned above. Historically, too, the family and authority structure valued, for reasons which were very good at the time, conformity and resistance to change. Now that change is happening, often at breathtaking pace, the young must be prepared, by their education, to come to terms with it, later ensuring that they can control their own lives as well as contribute constructively to their families' and their community's welfare. The education system and its curriculum have a great responsibility for this aspect of human development and every teacher must accept that he has a part to play in it, through his classroom activities and expectations.

Personal qualities

This is probably the most difficult area of essential education for the teacher to undertake. Fortunately it is the area in which the home and the local community make a major contribution. From them the children learn acceptable ways of behaving towards other people and property. They learn what natural impulses they must control and how to give them acceptable expression. Of course, not every home or community gives the same opportunity, and desired personal qualities and behaviours vary from family to family and community to community. Nevertheless, the school is part of the social world of its pupils and as such must make its own contribution to their personal development through its planned curriculum. This it can do through the ways in which the school is organized, by the rules that have to be followed, by the attitudes of the teachers towards their pupils, their colleagues at work and the activities in which the children are involved.

Once again, it is not possible to give rules which fit all

circumstances and every adult involved in education must make his own decisions about the personal qualities, attitudes and habits that his pupils need to be helped to acquire. If at all possible, the school's social structure and expectations from its pupils should reflect those which exist in their community. Things which are widely thought to be important outside the school should also be valued within it. This means that yet again, teachers should become as familiar as possible with the community and its social customs so that they can build on them and help their pupils to continue their personal development. Fortunately, following the principles of successful learning as outlined during the course of this book should fulfill most of the needs of the curriculum.

The 'hidden curriculum'

John Dewey, an American educator, wrote:
'Perhaps the greatest of all pedagogical fallacies is that a person learns only the particular thing that he is studying at the time'. (A *pedagogical fallacy* is a false belief about education and learning). It has been emphasised throughout this book that in schools, all sorts of hidden and unconsciously received 'messages' are being given to the learner which affect his learning and personal development. The attitudes of the teachers and the organization of the school itself, the things which are thought important, the prejudices which are widely held, the beliefs and expectations of the community at large, are all part of the learning environment of the school. They all have an effect on the pupils, whether we realise it or not.

The name given to these less obvious and usually unplanned learning experiences which exist in all schools and classrooms is known as the *hidden curriculum*. Because it is a reflection of the deeply ingrained concepts, attitudes, expectations and beliefs of the teachers, the educational authorities and the other pupils, the influence of the hidden curriculum is often overlooked. Since it is impossible to remove the incidental learning that stems from the hidden curriculum it is important that the teacher thinks very carefully about the forms that it might take in his own teaching, both in relation to all his pupils in general and to individuals in particular. He must ask himself what picture of each of his pupils he is giving them. What is he telling them about education, and learning and what things are considered valuable in them? What messages about other people, other language and ethnic groups, other age groups, is he delivering? What makes someone a successful person? The questions are endless.

It is hoped that working through this book has helped to make you more aware than before of the importance of the total educational context, not merely for the successful learning of the contents of the formal syllabuses in the curriculum but also for the achievement of the wider purposes of education. Much emphasis has been placed here on the total education of the *individual* in school rather than on the individual as a member of a particular culture group. This seems necessary because of the rapidity with which change is taking place throughout the developing world. It is not the school's role to determine the direction of that change, but to prepare those who are going to experience it most strongly to live within it and contribute constructively to it.

Application 23

a) Look back at all the previous Applications in this text and at your work in them. Would you now, after completing the book, make changes and additions to your earlier efforts? If so what would they be?
b) Discuss with a small group of fellow students what you think the author's own hidden curriculum includes, i.e. what else other than the content of and attitudes implied in the text have you learned from it? This is not an easy task and there are no right or wrong answers ... the author herself has found it difficult to identify her 'hidden curriculum'. But the attempt to do so should reinforce your awareness of this important aspect of successful education.

Further reading

Once again, Thompson (ibid) is a good source for you to build on when developing your own thinking about the curriculum relevant to your own country. The questions asked in the 'Suggestions for Further Study', (p. 333), are useful, especially if you answer them in the light of the knowledge of educational psychology which it is hoped that you have begun to acquire.

Index

ability: assessment of, 168-9; and self-concept, 123
abstract: motives, 73; reasoning, 65
accommodation (Piaget), 99
achievement, as grouping criterion, 43-4
activities, planning of, 136
adolescence, 57; and moral development, 146-7; problems of, 67-9, 184-7; and self-concept, 122; and traditional upbringing, 184-5
adolescent, development of, 62-70
age: as grouping criterion, 41, 42-3; uncertainty about, 52
age-related development, 38-40
aggressive behaviour, 127-8, 179-81 *passim*
aims, educational, 9
alcohol abuse, 186
anxiety, 125, *see also* motivation, negative
'apprentice master' teaching style, 151
aptitudes, assessment of, 168-9
arithmetic, 197-8
'army general' teaching style, 151-2
art, 199-200
assessment: continuous, 174-5; purpose of, 161-9; subjective, 169-70; techniques of, 169-76
assimilation (Piaget), 99
attainment, measurement of, 161-6
attention span, 51-2 *passim*, 83
attitudes, and self-concept, 123
authoritarian environment, and moral development, 147-8
authority and the teacher, 61

behaviour, change in, 185
behaviour modification, 139-40
Berry, and spatial reasoning research, 113
bilharzia, 59, 187
bilingualism, 196-7
Binet-Simon tests, 93-5
bullying, 179-80
'business man' teaching style, 152
'busy' work, 135

Certificate of Secondary Education, 164
change, in developing countries, 15-16
character, 119, 119
children, involvement with, 155-6
chromosomes, 24

205

classroom management, 135-8
clumsiness, during puberty, 63-4 *passim*
co-educational schools, 61, 123
cognition, 88-90
cognitive development (Paiget), 98-105; environmental effects on, 115-16; and language, 116-17
concrete operational stage, 102-4
conditioning, and moral development, 143
conformity, 54, 61, see also authority
conservative thinking, 115
continuous assessment, 174-5
conventional morality, 143
convergent thinking, 106
counselling, 178-9; in early primary education, 179-80; *see also specific problem*
creative thinking, 106, 115
creativity, 29, see also divergent thinking
cultural education, 199-200
cultural influences on personality, 119-20
cultural milieu, and education, 12
culture, literate, and the school entrant, 55
culture, and variability, 29-2
curiosity, and motivation, 75
curriculum, 189-92; hidden, 192, 202-3; modern, 192-4; objectives of, 195; principles of, 195-202

Dawson, and spatial reasoning research, 113
deficiency needs, 124
Deregowski, and pictorial material research, 114-15
developing countries, and educational psychology, 14-16
development: of adolescent, 62-70; age-related, 38-40; emotional, 46-7; intellectual, 46; physical, 38, 46; 6-12 years, 56-62; social, 46; *see also* stages, Piagetian
developmental patterns, 11-12, 38-9, 45-7
Dewey, John, *quoted*, 202
diagnosis, use of assessment tests for, 166-8
dialect, and language development, 53-4
dictionary, use of, 80
differences: compensation for, 21-2; observation of, 19-20
discipline, 121, 133-5; in classroom, 135-8; and high status pupils, 150; and moral development, 145-6; remedial measures for, 137-8; and self-actualisation, 126
discussion, and moral development, 146-7
disease, in 6-12 year olds, 59-60
disruptive behaviour, 127-8; in primary school, 179-81 *passim*
divergent thinking, 106, 115
drama, 199-200
drugs, 185-7

education, purpose of, 192-3
education, of teacher, continuing, 157-8
'Education for Living', 183
education psychology, and developing countries, 14-16; necessity of, 9-10; scope of, 10-11
emotional development, 46-7
engineers, and spatial reasoning, 114
environment: and learning, 25-6; and the personality, 119-20; and spatial reasoning differences, 107-8, 112-14
equilibrium (Piaget), 99
ethos of school, and self concept, 122-3
examinations, 60; public, 164-5,

(as social engineering, 166)
expectation: pupils', 79; of pre-school child, 54; of schooling, 60
experience, as facet of personality, 119
extended family, influence of, 30-1
eyesight, 57

fatigue: in 6-12 year olds, 59; and school performance, 52-3
Flanders, Ned, *quoted*, vii-viii
formal operational reasoning, 65, 104-5
free school (Zimbabwe), 44
functional invariants (Piaget), 99

g, 93, 105
Galton, Francis, and individual differences, 91-3
General Certificate of Education, 164
generation gap, 15, 66, 68, 200
genes, 24
genetic theory of intelligence, effect of on education, 95-6
genetic traits, 24-6
girls, underachievement of, 32-3
goals, *see* motivation
grouping, criteria for, 41, 42-4
groups, and discipline, 133-4
growth need, 124-5
growth patterns, 11-12
guidance, 178-9; in early primary education, 179-80; and employment, 182; *see also specific problem*
Guilford, on intelligence, 106

health, of teacher, 154-5
health education, 60, 199
height, determination of, 25
hidden curriculum, 192, 202-3
hookworm, 59
hormones, and temperament, 119

IQ (intelligence quotient), 94-5
illustrations, *see* pictorial material
impulsiveness, 127
individual differences: extrinsic, 28-34; intrinsic, 23-8
inheritance, genetic, 24-7 *passim*; and intelligence, 90-3
in-service courses, 157-8
intellectual abilities, 89, *see also* intelligence
intellectual development, 46; 6-12 years, 58-9
intellectual differences, and genes, 25-7
intellectual powers, and protein deficiency, 53
intellectual skills, development of, 200-1
intelligence, 89; and the environment, 96-7; inheritance of, 90-3; measurement of, 93-5; reduction of variability of, 29-30
intelligence A, B and C, 97
intelligence quotient, 94-5
intelligence tests, and Galton, 92-3
intelligence theory, effect of on education, 95-6
involvement, importance of, 1-2
isolated pupil, 125
isolation, in primary school, 181

knowledge: as aim, 9; integration of, 80, 89; of the teacher, 80-1
Kohlberg, on moral growth, 142-4
Kpelle, spatial reasoning of, 113-14

language: and cognitive development, 116-17; development of, 39; of instruction, 195-7; in pre-school years, 50, 51; second, 54
language development: and

207

dialect, 53-4; 6-12 years, 58-9
learned incompetence, 55-6
learning, 79-81; effect of environment on, 25-6; and past experience, 80; process of, 82-4; promotion of, 12; *see also* motivation
learning difficulties, in primary school, 181
learning potential, and genes, 25-6
lesson length, 83-4
lesson planning, and motivation, 74-5
literacy, 196-7 *passim*; and cognitive development, 115-16
literate culture, and the school entrant, 55
love, as a need, 124

MA (mental age), 93-4
malaria, 59
malnutrition, *see* nutrition
Maslow's need-achievement theory, 124-5; and classroom management, 137
mathematics, 197-8
maturity, *see* puberty
Mende, spatial reasoning of, 113
mental abilities, 26-7
mental age, 93-4
mental health of teacher, 154-5
misbehaviour, reinforcement of, 140
models, mental, 98-100, *see also* stages, Piagetian; self concept
moral development, 141-8; encouragement of, 146-7
morals, and discipline, 135
motivation: adult, 73-4; children's, extrinsic, 74-5; extrinsic, 73-5; and guidance programmes, 182-3; intrinsic, 75-6; negative, 76-7; positive, 77-8; *see also* expectation
multi-cultural societies, and educational psychology, 14-16

multiple choice tests, 172-4
muscle control, in 6-12 year olds, 56-7
music, 199-200
myth, 61-2

need fulfilment, 125-6
need-achievement, 124-5
noise, 135
normal distribution, 91
nuclear family: urban, 55; influence of, 31
number, and operational thinking, 102
number work, diagnostic tests for, 168
nursery schooling, 53
nutrition: and school performance, 52-3; in 6-12 year olds, 59

objective tests, 172-4
objectives, 79, 84-5, 85-6; as assessment tests, 161-2
observation of differences, 19-20
over-work, 127

parasites, 59-60, 187
parents, and individual differences, 30
participation, importance of, 1-2
pastoral care, 179
peer group: and the adolescent, 65, 66; and self-concept, 122
persistence, lack of, 127
personality, 118-19; development of, 121-6; and needs, 124-5; problems of, 126-8; of teacher, 128-9
personality traits: and the environment, 119-20; and genes, 27
physical development, 39, 46
pictorial material, 55, 114-15
planning: of activities, 136; of lessons, and motivation, 74-5
post-conventional morality, 143-4

practical experience, for 6 year olds, 51, 58-9
pre-conventional morality, 142-3
pre-operational stage, 101-2
pre-school experience, 53
protein deficiency, 53
psychological services, in behaviour problems, 180
psychology, defined, 8
puberty: in boys, 64; in girls, 63-4
public examinations, drawbacks of, 165
punishment, 139, 140-1; and negative motivation, 77
purpose, *see* objectives

questioning, 54
questions, design of, 170-4 *passim*

reading, technique of, 2
reading problems, 166-7
reading tests, 167
relationships, and concrete thinking, 103
relationships, mental, 101-2, 102-5 *passim*
religion: and moral development, 142; and personality traits, 120; and post-conventional morality, 144
reports, 175-6
rewards, 139
rules: and conventional morality, 143; reduction of and discipline, 136; *see also* discipline
rural children: arithmetic for, 197-8; knowledge of, 53; performance of, 16; teaching of, 156-7; and verbal ability, 69-70

schistosomiasis, 59-60, 187
School Leaving Certificate, 164
schools, and need fulfilment, 125-6
science, elementary, 198-9
science, and myth, 61-2

secondary education: experiental, 65; selection for, 44-5; enrolment area of, 69
security, for 6 year old, 51, 52
selection, 41, 42-4, 190; and genetic theory of intelligence, 95-6; *see also* streaming
self-actualisation, 124-6 *passim*
self-concept, 57-8, 121-3 *passim*; adolescent, 66; of teacher, 129
self-esteem, and discipline, 137
self-fulfilment, 124-6 *passim*
sensori-motor stage, 100-1
sex differences, 55-6; and single-sex schools, 61; in skills (6-12 year olds), 56
sex discrimination, and co-educational schooling, 123
sex roles, and the adolescent, 66-7
sexual maturity, *see* puberty
single-sex schools, 61
skills: as aim, 9; sex differences in, 56
smoking, 187-8
social contacts, in 6-12 year olds, 57
social development, 46; in 18 month-6 year old, 50-1
social engineering, public examinations as, 166
social scale, and the teacher, 150
social skills, 201-2, *see also* moral development
socialisation, discipline as, 134-5
'Socratic' teaching, 151
spatial reasoning, 69, 106-7; environmental effects on, 107-8; restriction in, 62; third world variations in, 112-14
stages, of moral development (Kohlberg), 142-4; examples of, 144-5
stages, Piagetian: concrete operational, 102-4; formal operational, 104-5; pre-operational, 101-2; sensori-

motor, 100-1
stages of development, 18 months-6 years, 49-56
streaming, 43—4; and end of year tests, 163-4; *see also* selection
study methods, 4-5, 82-4
subjective observations, 169-70
syllabus, and curriculum, 190-1
symbols, verbal, development of, 101

teacher: personality of, 128-9; preconceptions of, 33; self-concept of, 149-51 *passim*; study of role of, 12-13; variability reduction by, 29
teacher-training, and personality trait formation, 128-9
teaching: dissatisfaction with, 156; reasons for, 155; styles of (Thelen), 151-2
teaching post, first, 154-5
technical education, 198-9
technicians, and spatial reasoning, 114
Temne, spatial reasoning of, 113
temperament, 119, 119
test evaluation, 172
tests, 86-7; end of term/year, 162-3; objective, 172-4; teacher-made, 170-2; and vocational guidance, 184; *see also* examinations, assessment
Thelen, Herbet, and teaching styles, 151-2
'town manager' teaching style, 151
traits, as aims, 9
truancy, 181

urban children: knowledge of, 53; performance of, 16; variations in, 55

values, *see* moral development
variability, 29; increase of, 30-3; reduction of, 29-30
verbal ability, 69-70
verbal symbols, development of, 101
Vernon, Philip, on intelligence, 97
vocational guidance, 182, 183-4

Wolof, and cognitive development, 116

Zimbabwe, streaming in, 44

LIBRARY
SMCC Wythenshawe Park Centre
Moor Road
Manchester M23 9BQ